DEBORAH NEWTON'S cable collection

Rediscover your passion for knitting! These 19 refreshingly original sweaters, coats, and accessories by renowned designer Deborah Newton offer something for every creative mood and each fashion need. Whether you want to knit something casual, dressy, elegant, or fun, the 19 projects in this collection will delight you with stylish, curvy cables. Try your hand at knitting a cabled cardigan, handbag, or matching hat and fingerless gloves. Deborah loves to offer knitters such professional details as toggle closures, raglan sleeves, cap sleeves, and slit pockets—and in Deborah Newton's Cable Collection, you'll find all these exciting features and more!

LEISURE ARTS, INC.
Little Rock, Arkansas

EDITORIAL STAFF

Editor-in-Chief: Susan White Sullivan
Knit and Crochet Publications Director:
    Debra Nettles
Special Projects Director: Susan Frantz Wiles
Senior Prepress Director: Mark Hawkins
Art Publications Director: Rhonda Shelby
Technical Editor: Lois J. Long
Editorial Writer: Susan McManus Johnson
Art Category Manager: Lora Puls
Graphic Artist: Amy Temple
Production Artist: Janie Wright
Imaging Technicians: Brian Hall, Stephanie
    Johnson, and Mark R. Potter
Photography Manager: Katherine Laughlin
Contributing Photographers: Jason Masters
Contributing Photo Stylists: Angela Alexander
Publishing Systems Administrator: Becky Riddle
Publishing Systems Assistants: Clint Hanson
    and John Rose

BUSINESS STAFF

Vice President and Chief Operations Officer:
    Tom Siebenmorgen
Director of Finance and Administration:
    Laticia Mull Dittrich
Vice President, Sales and Marketing:
    Pam Stebbins
National Accounts Director: Martha Adams
Sales and Services Director: Margaret Reinold
Information Technology Director: Hermine Linz
Controller: Francis Caple
Vice President, Operations: Jim Dittrich
Comptroller, Operations: Rob Thieme
Retail Customer Service Manager: Stan Raynor
Print Production Manager: Fred F. Pruss

Library of Congress Control Number:
2009931392

ISBN-13: 978-1-60140-478-7
ISBN-10: 1-60140-478-6

contents

deborah NEWTON

Deborah Newton has truly earned her reputation as one of the top knitwear designers in the United States. She sold her first sweater to McCall's magazine in 1982 and has since designed and produced hundreds—perhaps thousands—of knitted garments. The skill she gained in an earlier career as a creator of stage costumes endows her work with dramatic flair and elements of fine tailoring. In 1992, Deborah

distilled her experience and knowledge into a book, *Designing Knitwear* (Taunton Press), an invaluable guide for the amateur knitter who wishes to create original patterns or simply improve their skills. The book remains in print nearly twenty years later, having attained the status of a classic. Deborah's work continues to appear in magazines and in book form. She also designs knitted fabrics for the Seventh Avenue garment trade.

Born in Rhode Island, Deborah has been a resident of Providence for over thirty years, where she lives with author Paul Di Filippo, her cocker spaniel Brownie, and her cat Penny Century. Perhaps her favorite place to relax in the world is the picturesque ocean haven of Block Island, although she admits that she has never yet designed a knitted bathing suit.

creative
CABLES

SIZES
To fit sizes Small{Medium-Large}.
Sample in size Small.

FINISHED MEASUREMENTS
Bust at underarm, buttoned: 42{47-52}"/106.5{119.5-132} cm
Length from back neck: 28{28^1/$_2$-29}"/71{72.5-73.5} cm

Size Note: Instructions are written for size Small with sizes Medium and Large in braces { }. Instructions will be easier to read if you circle all the numbers pertaining to your size. If only one number is given, it applies to all sizes.

"This jacket makes a bold statement in many ways. The combination of colorwork and cables is an interesting juxtaposition. And color enhances that! I chose autumnal colors-- but frosty shades, or beige-y neutrals, or even blacks and shades of grey would also work. The asymmetrical closure features the most perfect wooden toggles I could find. And a large collar, also placed off center, completes the strong look.

"This yarn is a mix of wool and mohair which has a springy quality that suits a large jacket. To change the look of the jacket entirely, you might eliminate the colored section entirely, just work the cabled pattern only. Or choose a very different yarn, like a metallic blend, to give the jacket a more dressy, less sporty, look."

5

MATERIALS

NASHUA HANDKNITS  [MEDIUM 4]
"Julia"
(50% Wool, 25% Alpaca, 25% Mohair; 50 grams/93 yards)
MC:
#NHJ.0178 (Harvest Spice): 19{21-23} skeins
CC:
#NHJ.0120 (Squash): 1{1-2} skeins
#NHJ.3961 (Ladies Mantle): 1{1-2} skeins
#NHJ.2163 (Golden Honey): 1 skein
#NHJ.0118 (Espresso): 1 skein
#NHJ.3158 (Purple Basil): 1 skein
#NHJ.6086 (Velvet Moss): 1 skein
#NHJ.4345 (Coleus): 1 skein
#NHJ.2083 (Magenta): 1 skein
Straight knitting needles, sizes
8 (5 mm) **and** 9 (5.5 mm) **or** sizes to obtain given gauges
Cable needle (cn)
Stitch markers
Yarn needle
2¼" (5.5 cm) Toggle buttons - 4
1" (2.5 cm) Toggle button

GAUGE

Cable and Rib Pattern with smaller needles:
28 sts and 22 rows = 4" (10 cm)
Colorwork Pattern with larger needles:
20 sts and 22 rows = 4" (10 cm)
Take time to save time, check your gauge.

PATTERN STITCHES

Front Cross (FC): Slip 4 sts to cn and hold in front, K4 from LH needle, K4 from cn.

CABLE AND RIB PATTERN:
Multiple of 14 sts plus 6
Rows 1 and 3 (RS): P2, K2, P2, (K8, P2, K2, P2) across.
Row 2 and all other WS rows: Knit the knit sts and purl the purl sts as they appear.
Row 5: P2, K2, P2, (FC, P2, K2, P2) across.
Rows 7, 9 and 11: P2, K2, P2, (K8, P2, K2, P2) across.
Row 12: Knit the knit sts and purl the purl sts as they appear.
Rep rows 1-12 for Cable and Rib Pattern.

P3, K3 Rib: Multiple of 6 sts plus 3
Row 1 (RS): P3, (K3, P3) across.
Row 2: K3, (P3, K3) across.
Rep rows 1-2 for P3, K3 Rib.

COLORWORK PATTERN: Use chart on page 11
Each square on chart represents one stitch *(see Fair Isle Knitting, page 124)*.
Begin and end pieces where indicated on chart.
Read odd-numbered RS rows from right to left, even numbered WS rows from left to right.

Note: Keep all edge sts, where noted, in St st.

Instructions begin on page 8.

BACK

With smaller needles and MC, cast on 158{170-186} sts.

Established Patterns (RS): K2 (edge sts), PM *(see Markers, page 124)*, beginning all patterns with Row 1, work P3, K3 Rib over 9{15-9} sts, PM, K2 (keep in St st), PM, work Cable and Rib Pattern over center 132{132-160} sts, PM, K2 (keep in St st), PM, work P3, K3 Rib over 9{15-9} sts, end k2 (edge sts).

Work even in patterns as established until piece measures approximately 9{10-11}"/23{25.5-28} cm, ending with Row 7 of Cable and Rib Pattern.

Purl WS row, decrease 53{53-57} sts evenly spaced *(see Decreases, pages 126 & 127 and Decreasing Evenly Across A Row, page 126)* — 105{117-129} sts.

Change to larger needles.

Colorwork Section (RS): Begin and end Row 1 of Chart, page 11, where indicated for Back.

Work even until piece measures 20" (51 cm), end with a WS row.

Armhole Shaping: Keeping in pattern, bind off 5 sts at the beginning of the next 2 rows.

Decrease 1 st at each end of the next 5{8-11} RS rows — 85{91-97} sts.

Work until Row 77 of chart is complete, end with a RS row.

Colorwork section should measure approximately 14" (35.5 cm).

Yoke Section (WS): With MC, purl WS row, increase 23{25-27} sts evenly spaced *(see Increases and Increasing Evenly Across A Row, page 126)* — 108{116-124} sts.

Change to smaller needles.

Established Patterns (RS): K2 (edge sts), (P2, K2) 0{1-2} times *(see Zeros, page 124)*, PM, work Row 1 of Cable and Rib Pattern over next 104 sts, PM, (K2, P2) 0{1-2} times, end K2 (edge sts).

Next Row (WS): P2 (edge sts), (K2, P2) 0{1-2} times, work Row 2 of Cable and Rib Pattern over 104 sts, (P2, K2) 0{1-2} times, P2 (edge sts).

Work even in patterns as established until armhole measures 8{8½-9}"/ 20.5{21.5-23} cm, ending with a WS row.

Back Neck and Shoulder Shaping: Mark center 20{22-24} sts.

Next Row (RS): Bind off 10{11-12} sts, work to marked sts and join a second ball of yarn, bind off center 20{22-24} sts, work to end.

Working both sides at the same time with separate balls of yarn, bind off 10{11-12} sts at the beginning of the next 5 rows AND AT THE SAME TIME, bind off 7 sts from each neck edge twice.

LEFT FRONT

With smaller needles and MC, cast on 63{69-77} sts.

Established Patterns (RS): K2 (edge sts), PM, beginning all patterns with Row 1, work P3, K3 Rib over 9{15-9} sts, PM, K2 (keep in St st), PM, work Cable and Rib Pattern over next 48{48-62} sts, PM, end K2 (edge sts).

Work even in patterns as established until piece measures approximately 9{10-11}"/23{25.5-28} cm, ending with Row 7 of Cable and Rib Pattern.

Purl WS row, decrease 26{26-28} sts evenly spaced — 37{43-49} sts.

Change to larger needles.

Colorwork Section (RS): Begin and end Row 1 of Chart where indicated for Left Front.

Work even until piece measures 20" (51 cm), end with a WS row.

Armhole Shaping (RS): Keeping in pattern, bind off 5 sts at the beginning of RS row.

Decrease 1 st at beginning of the next 5{8-11} RS rows — 27{30-33} sts.

Work until Row 77 of chart is complete, end with a RS row.

Change to smaller needles.

Yoke section (WS): With MC, purl WS row, increase 11{12-13} sts evenly spaced — 38{42-46} sts.

Established Patterns (RS): K2 (edge sts), (P2, K2) 0{1-2} times, PM, work Row 1 of Cable and Rib Pattern over next 34 sts, PM, K2 (edge sts).

Next Row (WS): P2 (edge sts), work Row 2 of Cable and Rib Pattern over next 34 sts, (P2, K2) 0{1-2} times, end P2 (edge sts).

Work even in patterns as established until armhole measures 6{6$\frac{1}{2}$-7}"/ 15{16.5-18} cm, end with a RS row.

Neck Shaping: Bind off 2{3-3} sts at the beginning of the row, then 2{2-3} sts at the beginning of the next WS row — 34{37-40} sts.

Next (decrease) Row (RS): Work to last 3 sts, K2 tog, K1 — 33{36-39} sts.

Work WS row as established.

Rep the last 2 rows 3 times more — 30{33-36} sts.

Shoulder Shaping (RS): Bind off 10{11-12} sts at the beginning of the next 3 RS rows.

RIGHT FRONT
Work same as for Left Front reversing placement of patterns and all shaping, beginning and end Colorwork chart where indicated for Right Front.

SLEEVES
With smaller needles and MC, cast on 66 sts.

Established Patterns (RS): K2 (edge sts), PM, work Row 1 of Cable and Rib Pattern over center 62 sts, end K2 (edge sts).

Work even for 5 rows.

Next (increase) Row (RS): K2 (edge sts), M1-p *(Fig. 7, page 126)*, work to last 2 sts, M1-p, K2 (edge sts).

Working increases into P3, K3 Rib, rep increase row every 6th row 14{4-0} times more, every 4th row 2{17-20} times, then every 2nd row 0{0-6} times — 100{110-120} sts.

Cap Shaping: Bind off 5 sts at the beginning of the next 2 rows, 2 sts at the beginning of the next 32{32-34} rows, then 1{3-3} sts at beginning of next 2{4-6} rows.

Bind off remaining 24 sts.

LEFT FRONT PANEL
With smaller needle and MC, cast on 52 sts.

Established Patterns (RS): K2 (edge sts), PM, work Row 1 of Cable and Rib Pattern over center 48 sts, PM, K2 (edge sts).

Work even until piece measures 24{24$\frac{1}{2}$-25}"/61{62-63.5} cm, end with a RS row.

Neck Shaping (WS): Bind off from beginning of WS rows 28 sts once, then 4 sts 6 times.

RIGHT FRONT PANEL
Work same as for Left Front Panel, reversing neck shaping.

FINISHING
Sew Fronts to Back at shoulders.

Weave side seams *(Fig. 14, page 128)*.

Sew Right Front panel to Right Front.

Sew Left Front panel to Left Front.

Left Panel (inner) trim: With smaller needles and RS facing, pick up 109{112-115} sts evenly along edge *(Fig. 13a, page 128)*.

Next Row (WS): Knit to the last 6 sts, make a 3-st buttonhole (by binding off 3 sts and casting on 3 sts while working bind off row), K3.

Bind off on next row.

Instructions continued on page 10.

Right Panel (outer) trim: With smaller needles and RS facing, pick up 109{112-115} sts evenly along edge.

Next Row (WS): K3, (make a 3-st buttonhole, K 22) 4 times, (by binding off 3 sts and casting on 3 sts while working bind off row), knit across to end.

Bind off.

Inner ties (make 2): With smaller needles, cast on 75 sts.

Bind off.

Sew first tie at the outside edge of Left Front Panel at waist, and second tie on wrong side of inner Right Front Panel at seam, even with first tie.

Sew smaller button to wrong side of inner Right Front Panel opposite buttonhole.

Sew larger buttons to Left Front opposite buttonholes.

Collar: With smaller needles and MC, cast on 158{170-182} sts.

Established Patterns (RS): K2 (edge sts), PM, beginning all patterns with Row 1, work P3, K3 Rib over 9{15-21} sts, PM, K2 (keep in St st), PM, work Cable and Rib Pattern over center 132 sts, PM, K2 (keep in St st), PM, work P3, K3 Rib over 9{15-21} sts, K2 (edge sts).

Work even in patterns as established until piece measures approximately 6-7" (15-18 cm), ending with Row 7 of Cable and Rib Pattern.

Neckline Shaping (WS): Bind off 9{10-11} sts at the beginning of the next 12 rows.

Bind off remaining 50 sts.

Sew cast on edge of collar in place around neck edge.

Weave Sleeve seams.

Sew Sleeve caps into armholes.

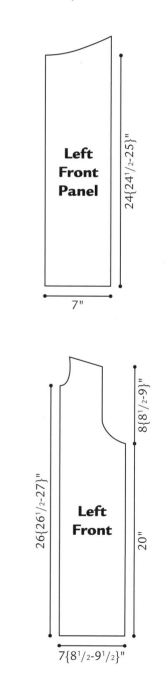

Left Front Panel

24{24½-25}"

7"

Left Front

26{26½-27}"

8{8½-9}"

20"

7{8½-9½}"

Sleeve

14{15½-17}"

5{5½-6}"

17½"

9½"

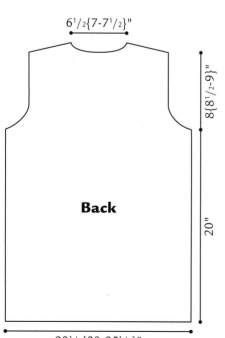

Back

6½{7-7½}"

8{8½-9}"

20"

20½{23-25½}"

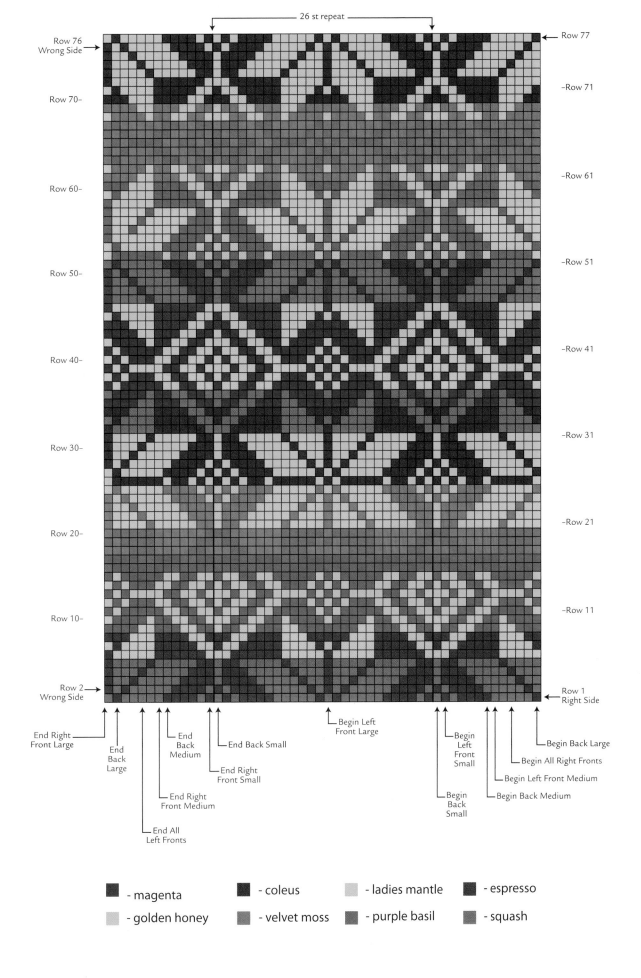

26 st repeat

Row 76 Wrong Side → ← Row 77
Row 70– –Row 71
Row 60– –Row 61
–Row 51
Row 50–
Row 40– –Row 41
–Row 31
Row 30–
Row 20– –Row 21
Row 10– –Row 11
Row 2 Wrong Side → ← Row 1 Right Side

End Right Front Large
End Back Large
End All Left Fronts
End Right Front Medium
End Back Medium
End Right Front Small
End Back Small
Begin Left Front Large
Begin Back Small
Begin Left Front Small
Begin Back Medium
Begin Left Front Medium
Begin All Right Fronts
Begin Back Large

■ - magenta
■ - golden honey
■ - coleus
■ - velvet moss
■ - ladies mantle
■ - purple basil
■ - espresso
■ - squash

11

cabled
CONFECTION

◖■■▭ INTERMEDIATE

SIZES
To fit sizes Small{Medium-Large}.
Sample in size Small.

FINISHED MEASUREMENTS
Bust at underarm, buttoned:
41{45-49}"/104{114.5-124.5} cm
Length from back neck:
28{28^1/$_2$-29}"/71{72.5-73.5} cm

Size Note: Instructions are written for size Small with sizes
Medium and Large in braces { }. Instructions will be easier
to read if you circle all the numbers pertaining to your size.
If only one number is given, it applies to all sizes.

"I have always loved mohair yarns for specialty winter garments. Mohair has body
but lightness, and the halo of fibers in the yarn catches the light and makes any
sweater in any color just glow.

"This swing-shaped jacket is oversized for drama in all aspects—body, hood and
sleeves. The cables are large and bold. All this lends, I hope, the perfect look well
suited for ice skating, winter holidays, or a special event. I found large mother of
pearl buttons as luminous as the aqua mohair."

MATERIALS
CLASSIC ELITE
"La Gran"
(76½% Mohair, 17½% Wool, 6% Nylon;
42 grams/ 90 yards)
Color #6567 (Aqua):
18{20-22} skeins
Straight knitting needles,
size 9 (5.5 mm) **or** size
needed to obtain gauge
36" (91.5 cm) Circular knitting
needle, size 9 (5.5 mm)
Cable needle (cn)
Stitch markers
Yarn needle
1½" (4 cm) Buttons - 4

GAUGE
Over St st: 16 sts and 22 rows = 4"
(10 cm)
Cabled Panel over 26 sts
measures approximately 5"
(12.5 cm)
Back Cross Cable over 12 sts
measures approximately 2" (5 cm)
Take time to save time, check your
gauge.

PATTERN STITCHES
Back Cross (BC): Slip 2 sts to cn and hold in back, K2 from LH needle, K2 from cn.
Cross 5 Back (C5B): Slip 5 sts to cn and hold in back, K5 from LH needle, K5 from cn.
Cross 5 Front (C5F): Slip 5 sts to cn and hold in front, K5 from LH needle, K5 from cn.
Twist 3 Back (T3B): Slip 1 st to cn and hold in back, K2 from LH needle, P1 from cn.
Twist 3 Front (T3F): Slip 2 sts to cn and hold in front, P1 from LH needle, K2 from cn.

K3, P2 RIB: Multiple of 5 sts plus 3
Row 1 (RS): K3, (P2, K3) across.
Row 2: P3, (K2, P3) across.
Rep Rows 1 and 2 for K3, P2 Rib.

STOCKINETTE STITCH (St st): Any number of sts
Knit RS rows, purl WS rows.

REVERSE STOCKINETTE STITCH (Rev St st): Any number of sts
Purl RS rows, knit WS rows.

BACK CROSS CABLE: Over 12 sts
Rows 1, 3 and 5 (RS): P1, K 10, P1.
Row 2 and all other even numbered WS rows: K1, P 10, K1.
Row 7: P1, C5B, P1.
Rows 9, 11, 13: P1, K 10, P1.
Row 14: K1, P 10, K1.
Rep Rows 1-14 for Back Cross Cable.

FRONT CROSS CABLE: Over 12 sts
Same as for Back Cross Cable except:
Row 7: P1, C5F, P1.
Rep Rows 1-14 Front Cross Cable.

CABLED PATTERN: Over 26 sts
Row 1 (RS): P5, K4, P8, K4, P5.
Row 2: K5, P4, K8, P4, K5.
Row 3: P5, BC, P8, BC, P5.
Row 4: K5, P4, K8, P4, K5.
Row 5: P4, T3B, T3F, P6, T3B, T3F, P4.
Row 6: K4, P2, K2, P2, K6, P2, K2, P2, K4.
Row 7: P3, T3B, P2, T3F, P4, T3B, P2, T3F, P3.
Row 8: K3, P2, (K4, P2) across to last 3 sts, K3.
Row 9: P2, (T3B, P4, T3F) across.
Row 10: K2, (P2, K6, P2, K2) across.
Row 11: P1, (T3B, P6, T3F) across to last st, P1.
Row 12: K1, P2, K8, P4, K8, P2, K1.
Row 13: P1, K2, P8, BC, P8, K2, P1.
Row 14: K1, P2, K8, P4, K8, P2, K1.
Row 15: P1, K2, P8, K4, P8, K2, P1.

Row 16: K1, P2, K8, P4, K8, P2, K1.
Row 17: P1, K2, P8, BC, P8, K2, P1.
Row 18: K1, P2, K8, P4, K8, P2, K1.
Row 19: P1, (T3F, P6, T3B) across to last st, P1.
Row 20: K2, (P2, K6, P2, K2) across.
Row 21: P2, (T3F, P4, T3B, P2) across.
Row 22: K3, P2, (K4, P2) across to last 3 sts, K3.
Row 23: P3, T3F, P2, T3B, P4, T3F, P2, T3B, P3.
Row 24: K4, P2, K2, P2, K6, P2, K2, P2, K4.
Row 25: P4, T3F, T3B, P6, T3F, T3B, P4.
Row 26: K5, P4, K8, P4, K5.
Row 27: P5, BC, P8, BC, P5.
Row 28: K5, P4, K8, P4, K5.
Rep Rows 1-28 for Cabled Pattern.

Note: Keep all edge sts, where noted, in St st.

Instructions begin on page 16.

BACK

Cast on 148{158-168} sts.

Established Rib Patterns (RS): Beginning with Row 1 of all patterns, work K3, P2 Rib over 13{18-23} sts, PM *(see Markers, page 124)*, work Front Cross Cable over 12 sts, PM, work K3, P2 Rib over 33 sts, PM, work Front Cross Cable over 12 sts, PM, work K3, P2 Rib over center 8 sts, PM, work Back Cross Cable over 12 sts, PM, work K3, P2 Rib over 33 sts, PM, work Back Cross Cable over 12 sts, PM, work K3, P2 Rib over remaining 13{18-23} sts.

Work even until piece measures 4" (10 cm), end with a RS row.

Next Row (WS):
P 13{18-23} sts AND AT THE SAME TIME, decrease 5{6-7} sts evenly spaced before marker *(see Decreases, pages 126 & 127 and Decreasing Evenly Across A Row, page 126)* (now 8{12-16} sts in this section), slip marker, continue Cable over 12 sts, slip marker, purl 33 sts AND AT THE SAME TIME, increase 1 st evenly spaced before marker *(see Increases and Increasing Evenly Across A Row, page 126)* (now 34 sts in this section), slip marker, continue Cable over 12 sts, slip marker, purl 8 sts AND AT THE SAME TIME, decrease 2 sts evenly spaced before marker (now 6 sts in this center section), slip marker, continue Cable over 12 sts, slip marker, P 33 sts AND AT THE SAME TIME, increase 1 st evenly spaced before marker (now 34 sts in this section), slip marker, continue Cable over 12 sts, slip marker, P 13{18-23} sts AND AT THE SAME TIME, decrease 5{6-7} sts evenly spaced before end of row (now 8{12-16} sts in this section) — 138{146-154} sts.

Established Patterns (RS):
Work 8{12-16} sts in St st, slip marker, continue Cable over 12 sts, slip marker, work 4 sts in Rev St st, PM, work row 1 of Cabled Pattern over 26 sts, PM, work 4 sts in Rev St st, slip marker, continue Cable over 12 sts, slip marker, work center 6 sts in St st, slip marker, continue Cable over 12 sts, slip marker, work 4 sts in Rev St st, PM, work row 1 of Cabled Pattern over 26 sts, PM, work 4 sts in Rev St st, slip marker, continue Cable over 12 sts, slip marker, work remaining 8{12-16} sts in St st.

Work even in patterns as established for 17 more rows, end with a WS row.

Next (decrease) Row (RS):
K2, SSK *(Figs. 11a-c, page 127)*, work to marker, slip marker, continue Cable over 12 sts, slip marker, decrease 1 in next section by P2 tog *(Fig. 9, page 127)*, slip marker, continue Cabled Pattern over 26 sts, slip marker, decrease 1 in next section by P2 tog, slip marker, continue Cable over 12 sts, slip marker, purl center 6 sts, slip marker, continue Cable over 12 sts, slip marker, decrease 1 in next section by P2 tog, slip marker, continue Cabled Pattern over 26 sts, slip marker, decrease 1 in next section by P2 tog, slip marker, continue Cable over 12 sts, slip marker, work to last 4 sts, K2 tog *(Fig. 8, page 126)*, K2 — 132{140-148} sts.

Keeping in patterns as established, rep decrease row every 18th row 3 times more — 114{122-130} sts.

Note: On last decrease row it may be necessary to remove adjacent markers to work last decreases.

Work even in patterns as established until piece measures 20" (51 cm), end with a WS row.

Instructions continued on page 18.

Armhole Shaping: Bind off 4 sts at the beginning of the next 2 rows, then bind off 2 sts at the beginning of the next 10{12-14} rows — 86{90-94} sts.

Keeping first and last 2 sts in St st, work even in patterns until armhole measures 8{8^1/$_2$-9}"/ 20.5{21.5-23} cm, end with a WS row.

Back Neck and Shoulder Shaping: Mark center 22 sts.

Next Row: Bind off 7{8-9} sts, work to marked sts and join a second ball of yarn, bind off center 22 sts work to end.

Working both sides at the same time with separate balls of yarn, bind off 7{8-9} sts at beginning of next 3{5-3} rows, then 8{0-8} sts at beginning of next 2 rows *(see Zeros, page 124)* AND AT THE SAME TIME, bind off from each neck edge 5 sts twice.

LEFT FRONT

Cast on 72{77-82} sts.

Established Rib Patterns (RS): Beginning with Row 1 of all patterns, work K3, P2 Rib over 13{18-23} sts, PM, work Front Cross Cable over 12 sts, PM, work K3, P2 Rib over 33 sts, PM, work Front Cross Cable over 12 sts, PM, end K2 (edge sts).

Work even until piece measures 4" (10 cm), end with a RS row.

Next Row (WS): P2 (edge sts), slip marker, continue Cable over 12 sts, slip marker, P 33 sts AND AT THE SAME TIME, increase 1 st evenly spaced before marker (now 34 sts in this section), slip marker, continue Cable over 12 sts, slip marker, P 13{18-23} sts AND AT THE SAME TIME decrease 5{6-7} sts evenly spaced before end of row (now 8{12-16} sts in this section) — 68{72-76} sts.

Established Patterns (RS): Work 8{12-16} sts in St st, slip marker, continue Cable over 12 sts, slip marker, work 4 sts in Rev St st, PM, work Row 1 of Cabled Pattern over 26 sts, PM, work 4 sts in Rev St st, slip marker, continue Cable over 12 sts, slip marker, end K2 (edge sts).

Work even in patterns as established for 17 more rows, end with a WS row.

Next (decrease) Row (RS): K2, SSK, work to marker, slip marker, continue Cable over 12 sts, slip marker, decrease 1 in next section by P2 tog, slip marker, continue Cabled Pattern over 26 sts, slip marker, decrease 1 in next section by P2 tog, slip marker, continue Cable over 12 sts, slip marker, end K2 (edge sts).

Keeping in patterns as established, rep decrease row every 18th row 3 times more — 56{60-64} sts.

Note: On last decrease row it may be necessary to remove adjacent markers to work last decreases.

Work even in patterns as established until piece measures 20" (51 cm), end with a WS row.

Armhole Shaping (RS): Bind off 4 sts at the beginning of the next row, then 2 sts at the beginning of the next 5{6-7} RS rows — 42{44-46} sts.

Work in pattern as established until armhole measures 6{6½-7}"/15{16.5-18}, end with a RS row.

Neck Shaping (WS): Bind off 10 sts once, then 2 sts 5 times — 22{24-26} sts.

Work even until armhole measures 8{8½-9}"/20.5{21.5-23} cm, end with a WS row.

Shoulder Shaping (RS): Bind off 7{8-9} sts at the beginning of the next 2{3-2} RS rows, then 8{0-8} sts on the last RS row.

RIGHT FRONT

Work same as for Left Front, reversing PATTERN placement and shaping and using Back Cross Cables instead of Front Cross Cables.

Instructions continued on page 20.

FIRST SLEEVE

Cast on 78 sts.

Established Rib Patterns (RS): Work in K3, P2 Rib over 13 sts, PM, work Row 1 of Back Cross Cable over 12 sts, PM, work in K3, P2 Rib over center 28 sts, PM, work Row 1 of Back Cross Cable over 12 sts, work in K3, P2 Rib over 13 sts.

Work even until piece measures 4" (10 cm), end with a RS row.

Next Row (WS): P 13 sts AND AT THE SAME TIME, decrease 6 sts evenly spaced before marker (now 7 sts in this section), slip marker, continue Cable as established, slip marker, purl center 28 sts AND AT THE SAME TIME, decrease 2 sts evenly spaced before marker (now 26 sts), slip marker, continue Cable as established, slip marker, P 13 sts AND AT THE SAME TIME, decrease 6 sts evenly spaced before end of row (now 7 sts) — 64 sts.

Established Patterns (RS): Work 7 sts in St st, slip marker, continue Cable over 12 sts, slip marker, work Row 1 of Cabled Pattern over center 26 sts, slip marker, continue Cable over 12 sts, slip marker, end work 7 sts in St st.

Work even in patterns for 11 more rows, end with a WS row.

Next (increase) Row (RS): K2, M1 *(Figs. 6a & b, page 126)*, work as established to last 2 sts, M1, K2: 66 sts.

Working increases into St st, rep increase row every 10th{8th-6th} row 5{7-9} times more — 76{80-84} sts.

Work even in patterns until Sleeve measure 17 1/2" (44.5 cm), end with a WS row.

Cap Shaping (RS): Bind off 4 sts at the beginning of the next 2 rows — 68{72-76} sts.

Next Row (RS): K2, SSK, work to last 4 sts, K2 tog, K2 — 66{70-74} sts.

Work WS row as established.

Rep last 2 rows 6{8-9} more times: 54{54-56} sts.

Bind off 2 sts at the beginning of the next 6{6-4} rows, then 3 sts at the beginning of the next 8{8-10} rows.

Bind off remaining 18 sts.

SECOND SLEEVE

Work as for first Sleeve, using Front Cross Cable instead of Back Cross Cable.

HOOD

Cast on 56 sts.

Established Patterns (RS): K3 (edge sts), work Row 1 of Back Cross Cable over 12 sts, PM, work Row 1 Cabled Pattern over center 26 sts, PM, work Row 1 of Front Cross Cable over 12 sts, end K3 (edge sts).

Work even in patterns for approximately 11 1/2" (29 cm), end with a RS row.

Keeping in patterns as established, working newly cast on sts in St st, cast on 45 sts at the beginning of the next 2 rows (90 sts total) — 146 sts.

Work even as established until newly cast on St st extensions measure 6" (15 cm), end with a WS row.

Bind off.

FINISHING

Sew hood together by joining cast on edge of St st sections to sides of Cabled section.

Sew Fronts to Back at shoulders.

Weave side seams *(Fig. 14, page 128)*.

Sew Hood in place around neck edge.

Front edging: With circular needle and RS facing, starting at lower right edge, pick up 112{115-117} sts along Front edge to neckline seam *(Figs. 13a & b, page 128)*, PM, pick up 175 sts along hood to left neckline edge, PM, then pick up 113{115-118} sts to lower Left Front — 400{405-410} sts.

Next Row (WS): (P3, K2) across.

Next Row (RS): (P2, K3) across.

Next (buttonhole) Row (WS): Work to marker at beginning of Right Front, slip marker, (work 20 sts, make a 3-st buttonhole) 4 times (by binding off 3 sts and casting on 3 sts on next row), work to end.

Work even until edge measures 1¹/₂" (4 cm).

Bind off.

Sew Sleeve caps into armholes.

Weave Sleeve seams.

Sew buttons opposite buttonholes.

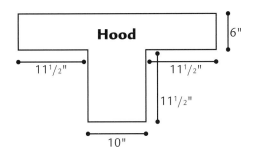

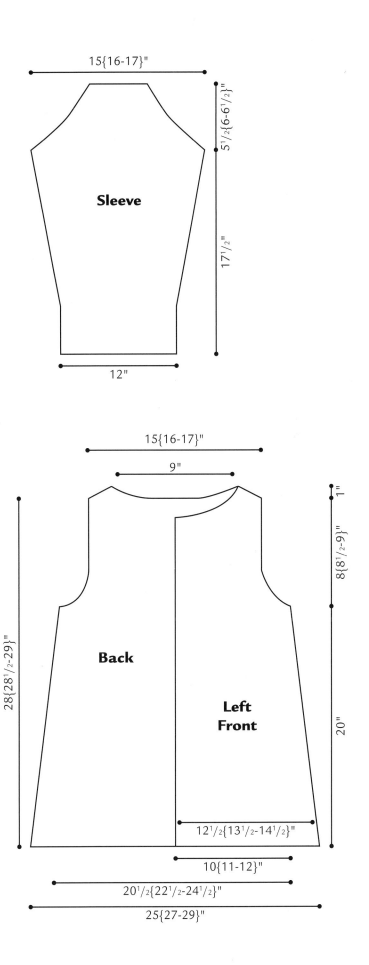

cultured
CABLES

◀■■■▷ INTERMEDIATE

SIZES
To fit sizes Small{Medium-Large-Extra Large}.
Sample in size Small.

FINISHED MEASUREMENTS
Bust at underarm:
40{44-48-52}"/101.5{112-122-132} cm
Length from back neck:
26{26^1/$_2$-27-27^1/$_2$}"/66{67.5-68.5-70} cm

Size Note: Instructions are written for size Small with sizes
Medium, Large, and Extra Large in braces { }. Instructions will
be easier to read if you circle all the numbers pertaining to
your size. If only one number is given, it applies to all sizes.

"I have always loved sweaters that zip! And why not use a zipper with a beautiful ring
detail, with an eye to the 1960's? And if one zipper is great—why not use three?

"To emphasize the long lean silhouette of this vest, I used a heavy drapey alpaca
yarn. The cables are simple, and so is the texture easy to knit. And I make sewing
the zippers in a little easier—stitches are picked up along edges to firm them. Then
the zippers can be pinned in and sewn by hand along the little 'dent' where the
stitches are picked up. I think you'll agree it is worth the extra effort..."

MATERIALS

REYNOLDS/JCA
"Andean Alpaca Regal"
(90% Alpaca, 10% Wool;
  100 grams/110 yards)
  Color #967 (Denim):
    8{9-10-11} skeins
Straight knitting needles, sizes 8
  (5 mm) **and** 10 (6 mm) **or** size
  needed to obtain gauge
Cable needle (cn)
Stitch markers
Yarn needle
25{25^1/$_2$-26-26^1/$_2$}"/
  63.5{65-66-67.5} cm long with
  ring-pull separating zipper
7" (18 cm) long closed end zipper
  with ring-pulls - 2
Note: Custom length zippers
  are available from:
  www.zipperstop.com
Sewing needle and matching thread
^{1}/$_8$ yard (.10 meters) fabric lining for
  pockets

GAUGE

Textured Pattern using larger needles:
15 sts and 24 rows = 4" (10 cm)
Take time to save time, check your
gauge.

PATTERN STITCHES

K3, P2 RIB: Multiple of 5 sts plus 2
Row 1 (RS): P2, (K3, P2) across.
Row 2: K2, (P3, K2) across.
Rep Rows 1-2 for K3, P2 Rib.

STOCKINETTE STITCH (St st): Any number of sts
Knit RS rows, purl WS rows.

REVERSE STOCKINETTE STITCH (Rev St st): Any number of sts
Purl RS rows, knit WS rows.

TEXTURED PATTERN: Odd number of sts
Row 1 (RS)**:** Knit across.
Row 2 (WS)**:** K1, (P1, K1) across.
Rep Rows 1-2 for Textured Pattern.

CABLE PANEL: Over 16 sts
Row 1 (RS)**:** P2, K 12, P2.
Row 2: K2, P 12, K2.
Row 3: P2, slip 3 sts to cn and hold in back, K3 from LH needle, then K3 from cn, slip 3 sts to cn and hold in front, K3 from LH needle, K3 from cn, P2.
Row 4: K2, P 12, K2.
Rep Rows 1-4 for Cable Panel.

LADDER PANEL: Over 12 sts
Row 1 (RS)**:** K2, P2, K1, P2, K1, P2, K2.
Row 2: P2, K2, P1, K2, P1, K2, P2.
Row 3: K2, P2, K1, P2, K1, P2, K2.
Row 4: P2, K2, P1, K2, P1, K2, P2.
Row 5: K2, P2, K4, P2, K2.
Row 6: P2, K8, P2.
Row 7: K2, P2, K4, P2, K2.
Row 8: P2, K2, P4, K2, P2.
Row 9: K2, P8, K2.
Row 10: P2, K2, P4, K2, P2.
Row 11: K2, P2, K4, P2, K2.
Row 12: P2, K8, P2.
Row 13: K2, P2, K4, P2, K2.
Row 14: P2, K2, P1, K2, P1, K2, P2.
Rep Rows 1-14 for Ladder Panel.

Note: Keep all edge sts, where noted, in St st.

Instructions begin on page 26.

BACK

With larger needles, cast on 101{111-121-126} sts.

Established Rib (RS): K2 (edge sts), PM *(see Markers, page 124)*, work Row 1 of K3, P2 Rib to last 2 sts, PM, K2 (edge sts).

Work even until piece measures 4" (10 cm), end with a RS Row.

Next (decrease) Row (WS): Purl, decrease 9{11-13-10} sts evenly spaced *(see Decreases, pages 126 & 127 and Decrease Evenly Across A Row, page 126)* — 92{100-108-116} sts.

Established Patterns (RS): K2 (edge sts), slip marker, work Textured Pattern over 15{19-23-27} sts, PM, work Ladder Panel over 12 sts, PM, work Cable Panel over 16 sts, PM, K2 (keep in St st), PM, work Cable Panel over 16 sts, PM, work Ladder Panel over 12 sts, PM, work Textured Pattern over 15{19-23-27} sts, slip marker, end K2 (edge sts).

Work even in established patterns until piece measures 16" (40.5), end with a WS row.

Armhole Shaping: Bind off 4{6-8-10} sts at the beginning of the next 2 rows — 84{88-92-96} sts.

Resume 2 edge sts on each end, and work as established until armhole measures 9{9^1/$_2$-10-10^1/$_2$}"/ 23{24-25.5-26.5} cm, end with a WS row.

Back Neck Shaping: Mark center 18 sts.

Next Row (WS): Work to center 18 sts, join a second ball of yarn and bind off center 18 sts, work to end.

Working both sides at the same time with separate balls, bind off from each neck edge 5 sts 4 times AND AT THE SAME TIME, when armhole measures 10{10^1/$_2$-11-11^1/$_2$}"/ 25.5{26.5-28-29} cm, end with a WS row.

Shoulder Shaping: Bind off 4{5-6-7} sts at beginning of next 4 rows, then 5 sts at beginning of next 2 rows.

LEFT FRONT

With larger needle, cast on 52{57-62-67} sts.

Next Row (RS): K2 (edge sts), PM, work Row 1 of K3, P2 Rib to last 3 sts, PM, work 2 sts in St st, 1 st in Rev St st (front edge).

Work even as established until piece measures 4" (10 cm), end with a RS row.

Next (decrease) Row (WS): Purl, decrease 4{5-6-7} sts evenly spaced — 48{52-56-60} sts.

Established Patterns (RS): K2 (edge sts), slip marker, work Textured Pattern over 15{19-23-27} sts, PM, work Ladder Panel over 12 sts, PM, work Cable over 16 sts, PM, work 2 sts in St st, 1 st in Rev St st.

Work even until piece measures 5" (12.5 cm), end with a WS row.

Pocket opening (RS): K2, slip marker, work Textured Pattern over 15{19-23-27} sts, slip marker, K2, P1 in first 3 sts of Ladder Panel for end of first section; join a second ball of yarn, P1 in next st, and continue second section in pattern as established to end of row.

Working both sections at the same time with separate balls of yarn, work in patterns as established until pocket opening measures 7" (18 cm), end with a RS row.

Close pocket (WS): Work as established across row with single ball of yarn.

Work even until Left Front measures 16" (40.5 cm), end with a WS row.

Armhole Shaping (RS): Bind off 4{6-8-10} sts at the beginning of the next row — 44{46-48-50} sts.

Resume 2 edge sts at beginning of row and work as established until armhole measures 7{7^1/$_2$-8-8^1/$_2$}"/ 18{19-20.5-21.5} cm, end with a RS row.

Front Neck Shaping (WS): Bind off 8 sts at beginning of WS row, then continue to bind off at Front neck edge 4 sts 2 times, 3 sts 3 times, then 2 sts 3 times AND AT THE SAME TIME, when armhole measures 10{10^1/$_2$-11-11^1/$_2$}"/ 25.5{26.5-28-29} cm, end with a WS row.

Shoulder shaping (RS): Bind off at shoulder edge 4{5-6-7} sts twice, then 5 sts once.

RIGHT FRONT

Work same as for Left Front, reversing placement of patterns, pocket opening and all shaping.

FINISHING

Sew Fronts to Back at shoulders.

Neckline ribbing: With larger needle and RS facing, pick up 138 sts evenly around neckline edge *(Figs. 13a & b, page 128)*.

Next Row (WS): P3, (K2, P3) across.

Next Row (RS): K3, (P2, K3) across.

Rep the last 2 rows for 2" (5 cm), end with a RS row.

Bind off AND AT THE SAME TIME, K2 tog in each K2 rib to keep rib from flaring.

Armhole ribbing: With larger needle and RS facing, pick up 83{88-93-98} sts evenly along armhole edge.

Work same as for neckline rib.

Bind off.

Weave side seams including ribbing *(Fig. 14, page 128)*.

Left Front Trim: With smaller needles and RS facing, beginning at top of neck rib, pick up 94{96-98-100} sts evenly along Front edge.

Bind off in knit on next row loosely so that edge does not draw in.

Rep on Right Front.

Weave in ends neatly away from Front edge.

Pin separating zipper in place so that trimmed edges just meet the zipper teeth and zipper teeth are not covered.

Sew by hand, in the ridge formed between the trim and the Front.

Pocket trim: With smaller needles and RS facing, pick up 30 sts evenly along one pocket edge.

Work as for Front trim.

Rep on second side of opening.

Join trims neatly where they meet and weave in ends away from trim.

Rep for second pocket opening.

Sew zippers in place.

Make fabric pockets and sew to inside of pocket opening.

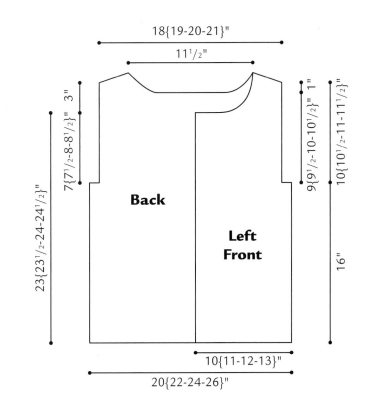

cabled
CACHET

■■■□ INTERMEDIATE

SIZES
To fit sizes Small{Medium-Large-Extra Large}.
Sample in size Small.

FINISHED MEASUREMENTS
Bust at underarm:
38{42-46-50}"/96.5{106.5-117-127} cm
Length from back neck:
14{14^1/$_2$-15-15^1/$_2$}"/35.5{37-38-39.5} cm

Size Note: Instructions are written for size Small with
sizes Medium, Large, and Extra Large in braces { }.
Instructions will be easier to read if you circle all the
numbers pertaining to your size. If only one number is
given, it applies to all sizes.

❖

"A cozy short bolero-type sweater like this works well year-round, in any fiber. If
you use a bouncy wool as I have here, the sweater has a lot of body; a softer, slinkier
yarn could lend a more drapey effect. The easy-to-remember allover pattern in the
body has a subtle small cable that repeats in a checkerboard fashion."

MATERIALS

TAHKI-STACEY CHARLES

"Torino Bulky"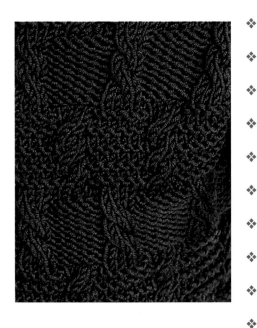
(100% Extra fine
Merino Wool;
50 grams/55 yards)
Color #249 (Dark Wisteria):
11{12-13-15} balls
Straight knitting needles,
size 10 (6 mm) **or** size
needed to obtain gauge
Cable needle (cn)
Stitch markers
Yarn needle
Sewing needle and matching
thread
1³/₈" (3.5 cm) Buttons - 3

GAUGE

Pattern st: 15 sts and 18 rows to
4" (10 cm)
Rev St st: 14 sts and 18 rows to
4" (10 cm)
To save time and ensure accurate
sizing, check gauge.

PATTERN STITCHES

Front Cross (FC): Slip 2 sts to cn and hold in front, K2 from LH needle, K2 from cn.
Back Cross (BC): Slip 2 sts to cn and hold in back, K2 from LH needle, K2 from cn.

STOCKINETTE STITCH (St st): Any number of sts
Knit on RS, purl on WS.

REVERSE STOCKINETTE STITCH (Rev St st): Any number of sts
Purl on RS, knit on WS.

CABLE PATTERN: Multiple of 10 sts plus 6
Rows 1, 3 and 7 (RS): P6, (K4, P6) across.
Rows 2, 4, 6, 8 and 10: K6, (P4, K6) across.
Rows 5 and 9: P6, (FC, P6) across.
Row 11: Knit across.
Rows 12, 14, 18, 20 and 24: Purl across.
Rows 13 and 25: P1, K4, (P6, K4) across to last st, P1.
Rows 15 and 23: K1, BC, (K6, BC) across to last st, K1.
Rows 16 and 22: K1, P4, (K6, P4) across to last st, K1.
Rows 17 and 21: Knit across.
Row 19: P1, BC, (P6, BC) across to last st, P1.
Row 26: Purl across.
Rep Rows 1-26 for Cable Pattern.

SLEEVE CABLE PANEL: Over 24 sts
Row 1 (RS): K4, P6, K4, P6, K4.
Row 2: P4, K6, P4, K6, P4.
Row 3: FC, P6, FC, P6, FC.
Row 4: P4, K6, P4, K6, P4.
Rep rows 1-4 for Sleeve Cable Panel.

Note: Keep all edge sts, where noted, in St st.
While working shaping, if unable to work entire cable, work in St st instead.

Instructions begin on page 32.

BACK

Cast on 74{82-88-96} sts.

Established Patterns (RS): K1 (edge st), work 3{2-5-4} sts in Rev St st, PM *(see Markers, page 124)*, beginning Cable Pattern and work over 66{76-76-86} sts, PM, work 3{2-5-4} sts in Rev St st, K1 (edge st).

Continue in patterns as established until piece measures 6" (15 cm), end with a WS row.

Armhole Shaping: Bind off 2 sts at beginning of next 6{8-8-10} rows, then 1 st at beginning of next 2{2-4-4} rows — 60{64-68-72} sts.

Resume edge st each side and work even until armhole measures 8{8^1/$_2$-9-9^1/$_2$}"/ 20.5{21.5-23-24} cm, end with a WS row.

Back Neck and Shoulder Shaping: Mark center 26 sts.

Bind off 3{3-5-5} sts, work to marker, join a second ball of yarn and bind off center 26 sts, complete row.

Working both sides at once, bind off 3{3-5-5} sts at beginning of next row, then 3{4-4-5} sts at beginning of next 4 rows AND AT THE SAME TIME, bind off at each neck edge 4 sts twice.

LEFT FRONT

Cast on 33{38-42-45} sts.

Established Patterns (RS): K1 (edge st), PM, work 5{0-4-7} sts in Rev St st *(see Zeros, page 124)*, PM, beginning Cable Pattern and work over 26{36-36-36} sts, PM, K1(edge st).

Continue in patterns as established until piece measures 6" (15 cm), end with a WS row.

Armhole Shaping (RS): Bind off 2 sts at beginning of next 3{4-4-5} RS rows, then 1 st at beginning of next 1{1-2-2} RS rows — 26{29-32-33} sts.

Resume edge st at armhole edge and work even until armhole measures 5{5^1/$_2$-6-6^1/$_2$}"/ 12.5{14-15-16.5} cm, end with a RS row.

Front neck shaping (WS): Bind off 5{6-7-6} sts at beginning of row.

Continue to bind off at neck edge (beginning of WS rows) 3 sts 3 times, 2 sts once, then 1 st once AND AT THE SAME TIME, when armhole measures same as Back to shoulder, bind off at shoulder edge 3{3-5-5} sts once, then 3{4-4-5} sts twice.

RIGHT FRONT

Cast on 33{38-42-45} sts.

Established Patterns (RS): K1 (edge st), PM, beginning Cable Pattern and work over 26{36-36-36} sts, PM, work 5{0-4-7} sts in Rev St st, PM, K1 (edge st).

Complete as for Left Front, reversing all shaping.

SLEEVES

Cast on 32{34-36-38} sts.

Established Patterns (RS): K1 (edge st), PM, work 3{4-5-6} sts in Rev St st, PM, work Sleeve Cable Panel over center 24 sts, PM, work 3{4-5-6} sts in Rev St st, K1(edge st).

Continue in patterns as established until piece measures 1" (2.5 cm), end with a WS row.

Next (increase) Row (RS): K1 (edge st), M1-P *(Fig. 7, page 126)*, work in patterns to last st, M1-P, K1 (edge st).

Working increases into Rev St st, rep increase row every 4th row 0{0-3-3} times, then every 6th row 8{9-7-7} times — 50{54-58-60} sts.

Work even until piece measures 14" (35.5 cm), end with a WS row.

Cap Shaping: Bind off 2 sts at beginning of next 2{4-4-4} rows, 1 st at beginning of next 6{2-2-0} rows, 2 sts at beginning of next 2{4-6-8} rows, then 3 sts at beginning of next 2 rows.

Bind off remaining 30 sts.

FINISHING

Sew Front to Back at shoulders.

Weave Sleeve and side seams **(Fig. 14, page 128)**.

Sew Sleeve caps into armholes.

Neckline trim: With RS facing, pick up 128{133-138-143} sts evenly along entire neck edge **(Figs. 13a & b, page 128)**.

Next Row (WS): P3, (K2, P3) across.

Next Row (RS): K3, (P2, K3) across.

Rep last 2 rows until trim measures 1¼" (3 cm), end with a RS row.

Bind off AND AT THE SAME TIME, K2 tog in every other K2 rib.

Left Front button band: With RS facing, pick up 51{53-57-61} sts along Left Front edge.

Established Seed st: K1, (P1, K1) across.

Rep this row until band measures 1¼" (3 cm).

Bind off.

Sew 3 buttons evenly spaced to band, the lowest 3" (7.5 cm) from bottom edge.

Right Front buttonhole band: With RS facing, pick up evenly along Right Front edge.

Work rib same as for neck edge AND AT THE SAME TIME, make three 3-st buttonholes opposite buttons on 2nd WS row (by binding off 3 sts and casting on 3 sts on next row), opposite buttons on Left Front button band.

Work until Band measures 1¼" (3 cm).

Bind off.

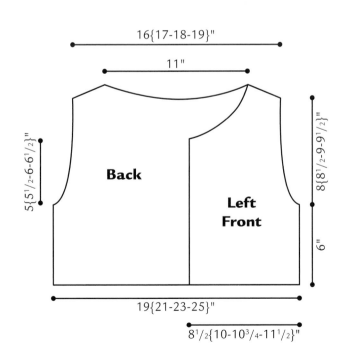

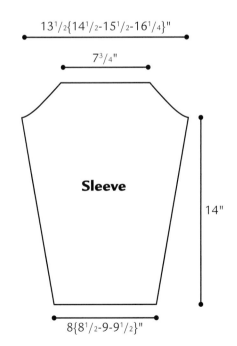

captivating
CABLES

 **INTERMEDIATE**

SIZES
To fit sizes Small{Medium-Large-Extra Large}.
Sample in size Small.

FINISHED MEASUREMENTS
Bust at underarm, buttoned:
36{40-44-48}"/91.5{101.5-112-122} cm
Length from back neck:
18{18½-19-19½}"/45.5{47-48.5-49.5} cm

Size Note: Instructions are written for size Small with sizes Medium, Large, and Extra Large in braces { }. Instructions will be easier to read if you circle all the numbers pertaining to your size. If only one number is given, it applies to all sizes.

❖

"This little swing-shaped cardi takes its texture from an easy allover cabled pattern that waves evenly over the knitted fabric. The simple garter stitch edges lend a sporty look. And the unshaped lower sleeves have a bell-effect.

"I love the contrast of two colors, but I can envision how pretty this would be in a solid colored yarn as well. For a dressier version, use a yarn with a slight halo of softness, one that has a touch of mohair or angora. I had been saving these vintage plastic buttons for a long time, finally matching them to this spice-colored yarn."

MATERIALS

CLASSIC ELITE
"Portland Tweed"
(50% Virgin Wool, 25% Alpaca, 25% Viscose;
50 grams/120 yards)
 A: #5085 (Yam):
  9{11-12-13} balls
 B: #5095 (Amaranth):
  1{2-2-2} balls
Straight knitting needles, size 7 (4.5 mm) **or** size needed to obtain gauge
24" (61 cm) Circular knitting needle, size 7 (4.5 mm)
Cable needle (cn)
Yarn needle
Sewing needle and matching thread
3/4" (19 mm) Buttons - 6

GAUGE

Over Wave Cable Pattern:
22 sts and 28 rows = 4" (10 cm)
Take time to save time, check your gauge.

PATTERN STITCHES

STOCKINETTE STITCH (St st): Any number of sts
Knit RS rows, purl WS rows.

WAVE CABLE PATTERN: Multiple of 8 sts plus 2
Row 1 (RS): Knit across.
Row 2 and all other WS rows: Purl across.
Row 3: K1, * K4, slip next 2 sts to cn and hold in front, K2 from LH needle, K2 from cn; rep from * across to last st, end K1.
Row 5: Knit across.
Row 7: K1, * slip next 2 sts to cn and hold in back, K2 from LH needle, K2 from cn, K4; rep from * across to last st, end K1.
Row 8: Purl across.
Rep Rows 1-8 for Wave Cable Pattern.

PARTIAL WAVE PATTERN:
Multiple of 8 sts plus 6
Work as for Wave Cable Pattern except:
Row 3: K1, * K4, slip next 2 sts to cn and hold in front, K2 from LH needle, K2 from cn; rep from * across to last 5 sts, end K5.
Row 7: K1, * slip next 2 sts to cn and hold in back, K2 from LH needle, K2 from cn, K4; rep from * across to last 5 sts, end slip next 2 sts to cn and hold in back, K2, K2 from cn, K1.

Note: Keep all edge sts, where noted, in St st.

Instructions begin on page 38.

BACK

Cast on 104{112-120-136} sts.

(With A knit 2 rows, with B knit 2 rows) 3 times.

With A knit 2 rows, increase 12 sts evenly spaced on last row *(see Increases and Increasing Evenly Across A Row, page 126)* — 116{124-132-148} sts.

Established Pattern (RS):
K1 (edge st), work in Wave Cable Pattern over center 114{122-130-146} sts, end K1 (edge st}.

Work even for 5 more rows, end with a WS row.

Side Shaping (decrease) Row:
SSK *(Figs. 11a-c, page 127)*, work to last 2 sts, K2 tog *(Fig. 8, page 126)*.

Keeping in pattern, making cable crosses whenever possible, even over partial number of sts if necessary, rep decrease row every 8th row 7{5-5-7} times more — 100{112-120-132} sts.

Work even until piece measures 12" (30.5 cm), end with a WS row.

Raglan Shaping: Bind off 4{4-5-6} sts at the beginning of the next 2 rows — 92{104-110-120} sts.

Next (decrease) Row (RS):
SSK, work to last 2 sts, K2 tog — 90{102-108-118} sts.

Rep decrease row every RS row 6{17-19-25} times more, then every other RS row 7{2-2-0} times *(see Zeros, page 124)* — 64{64-66-68} sts.

Bind off remaining sts.

LEFT FRONT

Cast on 54{58-62-70} sts.

(With A knit 2 rows, with B knit 2 rows) 3 times.

With A knit 2 rows, increase 6 sts evenly spaced (use backward loops) on last WS row — 60{64-68-76} sts.

Established Pattern (RS):
K1 (edge st), work in Wave Cable Pattern over center 58{62-66-74} sts (work Partial Wave Cable for size Medium), end K1 (edge st).

Work even for 5 more rows, end with a WS row.

Side Shaping (decrease) Row (RS): SSK, work to end.

Keeping in pattern, making cable crosses whenever possible, even over partial number of sts if necessary, rep decrease row every 8th row 7{5-5-7} times more — 52{58-62-68} sts.

Work even until piece measures 12" (30.5 cm), end with a WS row.

Raglan Shaping (RS): Bind off 4{4-5-6} sts at the beginning of row — 48{54-57-62} sts.

Work WS row as established.

Next (decrease) Row (RS):
SSK, work to end.

Rep decrease row every RS row 6{17-19-22} times more, then every other RS row 5{0-0-0} times more — 36{36-37-39} sts.

Bind off remaining sts.

RIGHT FRONT

Work same as for Left Front, reversing all shaping.

RIGHT SLEEVE

Cast on 62{70-78-86} sts.

(With A knit 2 rows, with B knit 2 rows) 3 times.

With A knit 2 rows, increase 6 sts evenly spaced (use backward loops) on last WS row — 68{76-84-92} sts.

Established Pattern (RS):
K1 (edge st), work in Wave Cable Pattern over center 66{74-82-90} sts, end K1 (edge st).

Work even until Sleeve measures 17" (43 cm), end with a WS row.

Raglan Cap Shaping:
Bind off 4{4-5-6} sts at the beginning of the next 2 rows — 60{68-74-80} sts.

Next (decrease) Row (RS):
SSK, work to last 2 sts, K2 tog — 58{66-72-78} sts.

Rep decrease row every RS row 6{13-15-17} times more, then every other RS row 5{2-2-2} times — 36{36-38-40} sts.

Top Shaping (RS): At the beginning of RS rows, bind off 6{6-8-8} sts 1{1-1-3} times, then 7 sts 4{4-4-2} times AND AT THE SAME TIME, continue to decrease at end of every other RS row 2 times more.

LEFT SLEEVE
Work same as for Right Sleeve, reversing top of cap shaping.

FINISHING
Weave Fronts and Back to Sleeves at raglan lines.

Weave side and Sleeve seams *(Fig. 14, page 128)*.

Striped Yoke: With circular needle, RS facing and A, pick up 27{27-28-30} sts along right neck *(Figs. 13a & b, page 128)*, 26{26-28-30} sts along top of Sleeve, 54{54-56-58} sts along Back neck, 26{26-28-30} sts along top of Sleeve, then 27{27-28-30} sts along left neck — 160{160-168-178} sts.

* Knit 1 row, knit 2 rows B, knit 2 rows A, knit 2 rows B, knit 1 row A, decrease 20 sts evenly *(see Decreases, pages 126 & 127 and Decreasing Evenly Across A Row, page 126)* — 140{140-148-158} sts.

Rep from * once more — 120{120-128-138} sts.

Knit 1 row A, knit 2 rows B, knit 2 rows A.

Bind off.

Left Front band: With RS facing and A, pick up 91{93-95-97} sts evenly along Left Front.

Knit 1 row, knit 2 rows B, knit 2 rows A.

Bind off.

Right Front band: Work same as for Left Front band, but work six 2-st buttonholes evenly spaced on first WS row as follows: K1, K2 tog, YO *(Fig. 3, page 125)*, SSK, (K 12, K2 tog, YO, SSK) 5 times, then knit to end. On next row, K1, P1 into each YO.

Complete as for Left Front band.

Sew buttons opposite buttonholes.

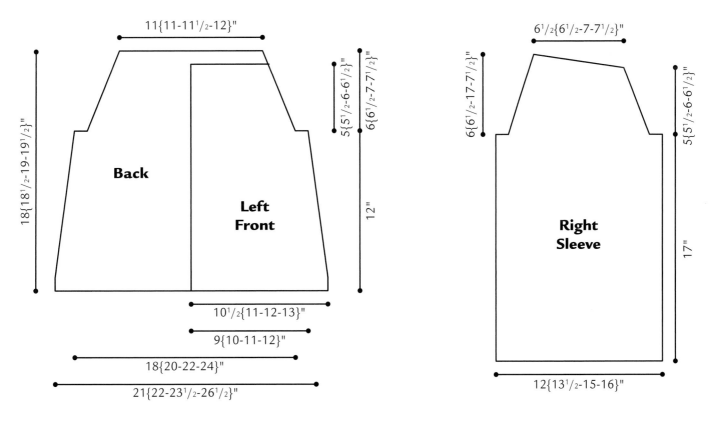

Colorful
CABLES

◖■■■◻ **INTERMEDIATE**

SIZES
To fit sizes Extra Small{Small-Medium-Large}.
Sample in size Small.

FINISHED MEASUREMENTS
Bust at underarm:
37{41-46-52}"/94{104-117-132} cm
Length from back neck:
25{25^1/$_2$-26^1/$_2$-27}"/63.5{65-67.5-68.5} cm

Size Note: Instructions are written for size Extra Small with sizes Small, Medium, and Large in braces { }. Instructions will be easier to read if you circle all the numbers pertaining to your size. If only one number is given, it applies to all sizes.

❖

"This long and lean pullover combines a yarn with interesting color variations with a chunky cable. Add on some simple texture at the sides, and you have a quick-to-knit and rewarding sweater.

"The design would work just as well in a solid colored yarn. For a more dramatic neckline, you could work the collar several inches more, even splitting it at center front."

MATERIALS

JCA/REYNOLDS "Smile"

SUPER BULKY 6

(72% Acylic, 28% Wool;
   100 grams/124 yards)
   Color #101 (Purple/Pink/
   Rust/Blue Multi):
   7{8-9-10} balls
Straight knitting needles,
   size 11 (8 mm) **or** size
   needed to obtain gauge
24" (61 cm) Circular knitting
   needle, size 11 (8 mm)
Cable needle (cn)
Stitch markers
Yarn needle

GAUGE

Broken Rib:
12 sts and 16 rows = 4" (10 cm)
24 st Cable Panel measures
approximately 4³/₄" (12 cm)
wide.
Take time to save time, check
your gauge.

PATTERN STITCHES

Front Cross (FC): Slip 3 sts to cn and hold in front, K3 from LH needle, K3 from cn.

Front Cross Purl (FCP): Slip 3 sts to cn and hold in front, P2 from LH needle, K3 from cn.

Back Cross (BC): Slip 3 sts to cn and hold in back, K3 from LH needle, K3 from cn.

Back Cross Purl (BCP): Slip 2 sts to cn and hold in back, K3 from LH needle, P2 from cn.

K2, P2 RIB: Multiple of 4 sts plus 2
Row 1 (RS): (K2, P2) across to last 2 sts, end K2.
Row 2: (P2, K2) across to last 2 sts, end P2.
Rep Rows 1 and 2 for K2, P2 Rib.

BROKEN RIB: Multiple of 4 sts plus 2
Rows 1, 3, and 5 (RS): (P2, K2) across to last 2 sts, end P2.
Rows 2, 4 and 6: (K2, P2) across to last 2 sts, end K2.
Rows 7, 9 and 11: (K2, P2) across to last 2 sts, end K2.
Rows 8, 10 and 12: (P2, K2) across to last 2 sts, end P2.
Rep Rows 1-12 for Textured Pattern.

CABLE PANEL: Over 24 sts
Row 1 (RS): P2, K3, P4, K6, P4, K3, P2.
Row 2: K2, P3, K4, P6, K4, P3, K2.
Row 3: P2, K3, P4, FC, P4, K3, P2.
Row 4: K2, P3, K4, P6, K4, P3, K2.
Row 5: P2, K3, P4, K6, P4, K3, P2.
Row 6: K2, P3, K4, P6, K4, P3, K2.
Row 7: P2, FCP, P2, K6, P2, BCP, P2.
Row 8: K4, P3, K2, P6, K2, P3, K4.
Row 9: P4, FCP, FC, BCP, P4.
Row 10: K6, P12, K6.
Row 11: P6, BC, BC, P6.
Row 12: K6, P12, K6.
Row 13: P4, BCP, FC, FCP, P4.
Row 14: K4, P3, K2, P6, K2, P3, K4.
Row 15: P2, BCP, P2, K6, P2, FCP, P2.
Row 16: K2, P3, K4, P6, K4, P3, K2.
Rep Rows 1-16 for Cable Panel.

Note: Due to the long color spacing, each garment will have an individual look. Join new balls in color section to create desired effect.

Instructions begin on page 44.

BACK

Cast on 54{62-70-78} sts.

Work in K2, P2 Rib for 4"
(10 cm), end with a RS row.

Next (increase) Row (WS):
Work 10{14-18-22} sts in rib as
established, PM *(see Markers,
page 124)*, mark next 14 sts,
purl these14 sts increasing 10 sts
as evenly as possible, PM, work
next 6 sts in rib as established,
PM, mark next 14 sts, purl these
14 sts, increasing 10 sts as evenly
as possible, PM, work remaining
10{14-18-22} sts in rib as
established — 74{82-90-98} sts.

Established Patterns (RS):
Beginning with row 1 of all
patterns, work 10{14-18-22} sts
in Broken Rib, work 24 sts in
Cable Panel, work center 6 sts
in Broken Rib, work 24 sts in
Cable Panel, work remaining
10{14-18-22} sts in Broken Rib.

Continue in patterns as
established until piece measures
19" (48.5 cm), end with a WS
row.

Raglan Armhole Shaping: Bind
off 5{6-6-6} sts at beginning of
next 2 rows — 64{70-78-86} sts.

Next (decrease) Row (RS):
K1, SSK *(Figs. 11a-c, page 127)*,
work to last 3 sts, K2 tog *(Fig. 8,
page 126)*, K1.

Keeping 2 sts each side in St st for
edge sts, rep decrease row every
RS row 10{11-12-10} times more.

Bind off 2 sts at beginning of
next 0{0-2-8} rows *(see Zeros,
page 124)*.

Bind off remaining
42{46-48-48} sts.

FRONT

Work same as for Back to Raglan
Armhole shaping.

Raglan Armhole Shaping: Bind
off 5{6-6-6} sts at beginning of
next 2 rows — 64{70-78-86} sts.

Next (decrease) Row (RS):
K1, SSK, work across to last 3 sts,
K2 tog, K1.

Keeping 2 sts each side in St st
for edge sts, rep decrease row
every RS row 7{8-8-6} times more
— 48{52-60-72} sts.

Bind off 2 sts at beginning of next
0{0-4-10} rows.

Bind off remaining
48{52-52-52} sts.

LEFT SLEEVE

Cast on 26{26-30-30} sts.

Work in K2, P2 Rib for 5"
(12.5 cm), end with a WS row.

Change to Broken Rib and work
for 6 rows.

Next (increase) Row (RS):
K2, M1 *(Figs. 6a & b, page 126)*,
work to last 2 sts, M1, K2.

Keeping 2 sts each side in St st for
edge sts and working increases
into Broken Rib Pattern, rep
increase row every 4th row
2{8-5-11} times more, then every
6th row 6{2-4-0} times —
44{48-50-54} sts.

Work even until piece measures
18" (45.5 cm), end on a WS row.

Raglan Cap Shaping: Bind off
5{6-6-6} sts at beginning of next
2 rows.

Next (decrease) Row (RS): K1,
SSK, work to last 3 sts, K2 tog,
K1.

Keeping 2 sts each side in St st for
edge sts, rep decrease row every
RS row 7{8-9-11} times more.

Continue to decrease at
beginning of RS rows 2 times
more AND AT THE SAME TIME,
bind off at beginning of WS rows
6 sts once, then 5 sts 2 times.

RIGHT SLEEVE

Work as for Left Sleeve, reversing
cap shaping.

FINISHING

Weave Front and Back to Sleeves
along raglan lines *(Fig. 14,
page 128)*.

Weave Sleeve and side seams.

Neckline Rib: With circular
needle and RS facing,
pick up 88{96-100-100} sts
evenly around neckline edge
(Figs. 13a & b, page 128); place
marker and join.

Work in rnds of K2, P2 Rib for 3"
(7.5 cm).

Bind off.

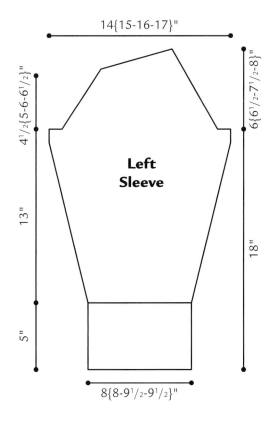

14{15-16-17}"

4¹⁄₂{5-6-6¹⁄₂}"

6{6¹⁄₂-7¹⁄₂-8}"

13"

**Left
Sleeve**

18"

5"

8{8-9¹⁄₂-9¹⁄₂}"

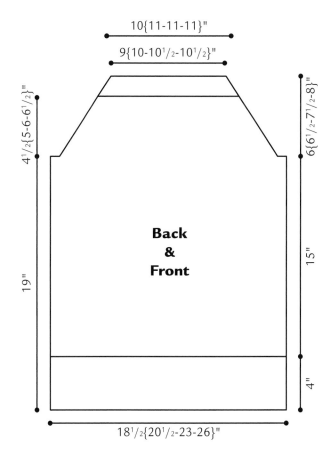

10{11-11-11}"

9{10-10¹⁄₂-10¹⁄₂}"

4¹⁄₂{5-6-6¹⁄₂}"

6{6¹⁄₂-7¹⁄₂-8}"

19"

**Back
&
Front**

15"

4"

18¹⁄₂{20¹⁄₂-23-26}"

collared
CABLES

◖■■■▭ INTERMEDIATE

SIZES
To fit sizes Small{Medium-Large}.
Sample in size Small.

FINISHED MEASUREMENTS
Bust at underarm:
39{43-48}"/99{109-122} cm
Length from back neck:
$19^1/_2${20-20$^1/_2$}"/49.5{51-52} cm

Size Note: Instructions are written for size Small with sizes
Medium and Large in braces { }. Instructions will be easier
to read if you circle all the numbers pertaining to your size.
If only one number is given, it applies to all sizes.

"This design was inspired by the lovely luminous yarn, a silk blend. How could I
achieve a slightly Asian feel? I planned an asymmetrical front closing like some
Chinese jackets. And I created a wide almost bell-shaped sleeve, bordered by the
cable pattern worked side to side. The allover cable pattern has a flatter texture
than some, with almost a 'brocade' quality.

This version is dressy in feel, but worked in a tweedy wool this sweater would have
a sportier look. For a summer version, try a thick and thin cotton or linen blend,
with a narrower ribbing at the neck."

MATERIALS

ELSABETH LAVOLD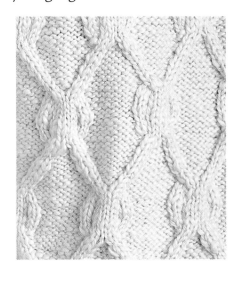
"Silky Flamme"

(50% Peruvian Wool, 30% FS Alpaca, 20% Silk; 50 grams/82 yards) Color #0002 (Ivory): 17{19-20} skeins

Straight knitting needles, sizes 9 (5.5 mm) **and** 10 (6 mm) **or** size needed to obtain gauge

Cable needle (cn)

Stitch markers

Yarn needle

Sewing needle and matching thread

1¼-1½" (3-4 cm) Buttons - 2

GAUGE

Garter Rib Pattern using larger needles:

15 sts and 24 rows = 4" (10 cm)

Cable Pattern using larger needles:

21 sts and 25 rows = 4" (10 cm)

Take time to save time, check your gauge.

PATTERN STITCHES

Back Cross (BC): Slip 4 sts to cn and hold in back, K4 from LH needle, K4 from cn.

Twist 4 Back (T4B): Slip 2 sts to cn and hold in back, K2 from LH needle, P2 from cn.

Twist 4 Front (T4F): Slip 2 sts to cn and hold in front, P2 from LH needle, K2 from cn.

Twist 3 Back (T3B): Slip st to cn and hold in back, K2 from LH needle, P1 from cn.

Twist 3 Front (T3F): Slip 2 sts to cn and hold in front, P1 from LH needle, K2 from cn.

STOCKINETTE STITCH (St st): Any number of sts
Knit on RS, purl on WS.

GARTER RIB: Multiple of 5 sts plus 3
Row 1 (RS): Knit across.
Rows 2: P3, (K2, P3) across.
Rep Rows 1 and 2 for Garter Rib.

CABLE PANEL: Multiple of 18 sts plus 2
Row 1 (WS): K6, P8, (K 10, P8) across to last 6 sts, K6.
Row 2: P6, T4B, T4F, (P 10, T4B, T4F) across to last 6 sts, P6.
Row 3: K6, P2, K4, P2, (K 10, P2, K4, P2) across to last 6 sts, K6.
Row 4: P5, T3B, P4, T3F, (P8, T3B, P4, T3F) across to last 5 sts, P5.
Row 5: K5, P2, K6, P2, (K8, P2, K6, P2) across to last 5 sts, K5.

Row 6: P4, T3B, P6, T3F, (P6, T3B, P6, T3F) across to last 4 sts, P4.

Row 7: K4, P2, K8, P2, (K6, P2, K8, P2) across to last 4 sts, K4.

Row 8: P3, T3B, P8, T3F, (P4, T3B, P8, T3F) across to last 3 sts, P3.

Row 9: K3, P2, K 10, P2, (K4, P2, K 10, P2) across to last 3 sts, K3.

Row 10: P1, (T4B, P 10, T4F) across to last st, P1.

Row 11: K1, P4, K 10, (P8, K 10) across to last 5 sts, P4, K1.

Row 12: P1, K2, T3F, P8, T3B, (K4, T3F, P8, T3B) across to last 3 sts, K2, P1.

Row 13: (K1, P2) twice, K8, P2, K1, (P4, K1, P2, K8, P2, K1) across to last 3 sts, P2, K1.

Row 14: P1, K2, P1, T3F, P6, T3B, P1, (K4, P1, T3F, P6, T3B, P1) across to last 3 sts, K2, P1.

Row 15: K1, P2, K2, P2, K6, P2, K2, (P4, K2, P2, K6, P2, K2) across to last 3 sts, P2, K1.

Row 16: P1, K2, P1, T3B, P6, T3F, P1, (K4, P1, T3B, P6, T3F, P1) across to last 3 sts, K2, P1.

Row 17: (K1, P2) twice, K8, P2, K1, (P4, K1, P2, K8, P2, K1) across to last 3 sts, P2, K1.

Row 18: P1, K2, T3B, P8, T3F, (K4, T3B, P8, T3F) across to last 3 sts, K2, P1.

Row 19: : K1, P4, K 10, (P8, K 10) across to last 5 sts, P4, K1.

Row 20: P1, (T4F, P 10, T4B) across to last st, P1.

Row 21: K3, P2, K 10, P2, (K4, P2, K 10, P2) across to last 3 sts, K3.

Row 22: P3, T3F, P8, T3B, (P4, T3F, P8, T3B) across to last 3 sts, P3.

Row 23: K4, P2, K8, P2, (K6, P2, K8, P2) across to last 4 sts, K4.

Row 24: P4, T3F, P6, T3B, (P6, T3F, P6, T3B) across to last 4 sts, P4.

Row 25: K5, P2, K6, P2, (K8, P2, K6, P2) across to last 5 sts, K5.

Row 26: P5, T3F, P4, T3B, (P8, T3F, P4, T3B) across to last 5 sts, P5.

Row 27: K6, P2, K4, P2, (K 10, P2, K4, P2) across to last 6 sts, K6.

Row 28: P6, T4F, T4B, (P 10, T4F, T4B) across to last 6 sts, P6.

Row 29: K6, P8, (K 10, P8) across to last 6 sts, K6.

Row 30: P5, T3B, K4, T3F, (P8, T3B, K4, T3F) across to last 5 sts, P5.

Row 31: K5, P2, K1, P4, K1, P2, (K8, P2, K1, P4, K1, P2) across to last 5 sts, K5.

Row 32: P4, T3B, P1, K4, P1, T3F, (P6, T3B, P1, K4, P1, T3F) across to last 4 sts, P4.

Row 33: K4, P2, K2, P4, K2, P2, (K6, P2, K2, P4, K2, P2) across to last 4 sts, K4.

Row 34: P4, T3F, P1, K4, P1, T3B, (P6, T3F, P1, K4, P1, T3B) across to last 4 sts, P4.

Row 35: K5, P2, K1, P4, K1, P2, (K8, P2, K1, P4, K1, P2) across to last 5 sts, K5.

Row 36: P5, T3F, K4, T3B, (P8, T3F, K4, T3B) across to last 5 sts, P5.

Rep Rows 1-36 for Cable Panel.

Note: Keep all edge sts, where noted, in St st.

Instructions begin on page 50.

BACK

With larger needles, cast on 112{122-132} sts.

Established Rib 1 (RS):
K0{1-2} *(see Zeros, page 124)*, (K2, P2) 4{5-6} times, K8, * P2, (K2, P2) 2 times, K8; rep from * across to last 16{21-26} sts, end (P2, K2) 4{5-6} times, K0{1- 2}.

Rows 2, 4 and 6 (WS): Knit the knit sts and purl the purl sts as they appear.

Row 3 (RS): K0{1-2}, (K2, P2) 4(5-6} times, BC, * P2, (K2, P2) 2 times, BC; rep from * across to last 16{21-26} sts, end (P2, K2) 4{5-6} times, K0{1-2}.

Rows 5 and 7: K0{1-2}, (K2, P2) 4{5-6} times, K8, * P2, (K2, P2) 2 times, K8; rep from * across to last 16{21-26} sts, end (P2, K2) 4{5-6} times, K0{1- 2}.

Row 8: Knit the knit sts and purl the purl sts as they appear.

Rep Rows 3-5, ending with a RS row.

Established Patterns (WS):
P2 (edge sts), PM *(see Markers, page 124)*, work Garter Rib over 8{13-18} sts, PM, work Row 1 of Cable Pattern over center 92 sts, PM, work Garter Rib over 8{13-18} sts, PM, end P2 (edge sts).

Work even as established until piece measures 3" (7.5 cm), end with a WS row.

Next (decrease) Row (RS):
K1, SSK *(Figs. 11a-c, page 127)*, work as established to last 3 sts, K2 tog *(Fig. 8, page 126)*, K1.

Keeping edge sts, rep decrease row every 10th row 4 times more — 102{112-122} sts.

Work even until piece measures 13" (33 cm), end with a WS row.

Raglan Armhole shaping:
Keeping in pattern, bind off 4{5-5} sts at the beginning of the next 2 rows — 94{102-112} sts.

For sizes Small and Medium only:
Next (decrease) Row (RS):
K1, SSK, work in patterns to last 3 sts, K2 tog, K1.

Next Row (WS): P2, work in patterns as established to last 2 sts, P2.

Rep last 2 rows 4{1- 0} more times.

For all sizes:
Next (decrease) Row (RS):
K1, SSK, work in patterns as established to last 3 sts, K2 tog, K1.

Next (decrease) Row (WS):
P1, P2 tog tbl *(Fig. 10, page 127)*, work in patterns to last 3 sts, P2 tog *(Fig. 9, page 127)*, P1.

Next (decrease) Row (RS):
K1, SSK, work in patterns to last 3 sts, K2 tog, K1.

Next Row (WS): P2, work in patterns to last 2 sts, P2.

Rep last 4 rows 6{8-9} times more.

For size Large only:
Next (decrease) Row (RS):
K1, SSK, work in patterns as established to last 3 sts, K2 tog, K1.

Next Row (WS): P1, P2 tog tbl, work in patterns to last 3 sts, P2 tog, P1.

Rep the last 2 rows one more time.

All sizes:
Bind off remaining 42{44-44} sts.

Instructions continued on page 52.

LEFT FRONT

With larger needles, cast on 32{37-42} sts.

Established Rib (RS): K0{1-2}, (K2, P2) 4{5-6} times, K8, (P2, K2) 2 times.

Rows 2, 4 and 6 (WS): Knit the knit sts and purl the purl sts as they appear.

Row 3 (RS): K0{1-2}, (K2, P2) 4{5-6} times, BC, (P2, K2) 2 times.

Rows 5 and 7: K0{1-2}, (K2, P2) 4{5-6} times, K8, (P2, K2) 2 times.

Row 8: Knit the knit sts and purl the purl sts as they appear.

Rep Rows 3-5, ending with a RS row.

Established Patterns (WS): P2 (edge sts), PM, work Row 1 of Cable Pattern over 20 sts, PM, work Garter Rib over 8{13-18} sts, PM, end P2 (edge sts).

Work even as established until piece measures 3" (7.5 cm), end with a WS row.

Next (decrease) Row (RS): K1, SSK, work as established to end.

Keeping edge sts, rep decrease row every 10th row 4 times more — 27{32-37} sts.

Work even until piece measures 13" (33 cm), end with a WS row.

Raglan Armhole Shaping (RS): Keeping in pattern, bind off 4{5-5} sts at the beginning of row.

Next Row (WS): Work as established to last 2 sts, P2.

For size Small only:
Next (decrease) Row (RS): K1, SSK, work in pattern to end.

Next Row (WS): Work as established to last 2 sts, P2.

Rep last 2 rows 4 times more.

For all sizes:
Next (decrease) Row (RS): K1, SSK, work in pattern to end.

Next (decrease) Row (WS): Work as established to last 3 sts, P2 tog, P1.

Next (decrease) Row (RS): K1, SSK, work in pattern to end.

Next Row (WS): Work as established to last 2 sts, P2.

Rep last 4 rows 4{7-3} times more.

For size Large only:
Next (decrease) Row (RS): K1, SSK, work in pattern to end.

Next (decrease) Row (WS): Work as established to last 3 sts, P2 tog, P1.

Rep last 2 rows 7 times more, then work RS decrease row once.

All sizes:
Bind off remaining 3 sts.

RIGHT FRONT

With larger needles, cast on 86{91-96} sts.

Established Rib (RS): (K2, P2) 2 times, K8, * P2, (K2, P2) 2 times, K8; rep from * across to last 16{21-26} sts, end (P2, K2) 4{5-6} times, K0{1-2}.

Rows 2, 4 and 6 (WS): Knit the knit sts and purl the purl sts as they appear.

Row 3 (RS): (K2, P2) 2 times, BC, * P2, (K2, P2) 2 times, BC; rep from * across to last 16{21-26} sts, end (P2, K2) 4{5-6} times, K0{1-2}.

Rows 5 and 7: (K2, P2) 2 times, K8, * P2, (K2, P2) 2 times, K8; rep from * across to last 16{21-26} sts, end (P2, K2) 4{5-6} times, K0{1-2}.

Row 8: Knit the knit sts and purl the purl sts as they appear.

Rep Rows 3-5, ending with a RS row.

Established Patterns (WS): P2 (edge sts), PM, work Garter Rib over 8{13-18} sts, PM, work Row 1 of Cable over next 74 sts, PM, end P2 (edge sts).

Work even as established until piece measures 3" (7.5 cm), end with a WS row.

Next (decrease) Row (RS): Work as established to last 3 sts, K2 tog, K1.

Keeping edge sts, rep decrease row every 10th row 4 times more — 81{86-91} sts.

Work even until piece measures 13" (33 cm), end with a RS row.

Raglan Armhole Shaping (WS): Keeping in pattern, bind off 4{5-5} sts at the beginning of row.

Instructions continued on page 54.

Next Row (WS): P2, work in patterns as established to end.

For size Small only:
Next (decrease) Row (RS): Work in pattern to last 3 sts, K2 tog, K1.

Next Row (WS): P2, work in patterns as established to end.

Rep last 2 rows 4 times more.

For all sizes:
Next (decrease) Row (RS): Work in pattern to last 3 sts, K2 tog, K1.

Next (decrease) Row (WS): P1, P2 tog tbl, work in patterns as established to end.

Next (decrease) Row (RS): Work in pattern to last 3 sts, K2 tog, K1.

Next Row (WS): P2, work in patterns as established to end.

Rep last 4 rows 4{7-3} times more.

For size Large only:
Next (decrease) Row (RS): Work in pattern to last 3 sts, K2 tog, K1.

Next (decrease) Row (WS): P1, P2 tog tbl, work in patterns as established to end.

Rep last 2 rows 7 times more, then work RS decrease row once.

For all sizes:
Bind off remaining 57 sts.

RIGHT SLEEVE
Cuff: With larger needles, cast on 42 sts.

Next Row (RS): K2 (edge sts), work in Cable Pattern over 38 sts, end K2 (edge sts).

Work even as established until piece measures 16{17-18}"/ 40.5{43-45.5} cm, end with a WS row.

Bind off.

Upper sleeve: With RS of cuff facing, pick up 62{67-72} sts evenly spaced across end of rows *(Fig. 13a, page 128)*.

Next Row (WS): P2 (edge sts), work in Garter Rib over 58{63-68} sts, end P2 (edge sts).

Work even for 4 rows more, end with a WS row.

Next (decrease) Row (RS): K1, SSK, work in pattern to last 3 sts, K2 tog, end K1.

Keeping edge sts, rep decrease row every 6th row 4 times more — 52{57-62} sts.

Work even until Sleeve measures 5" (12.5 cm) above cuff, end with a WS row.

Raglan cap shaping: Keeping in pattern, bind off 4{5-5} sts at the beginning of the next 2 rows.

Work 2 rows even.

For sizes Small and Medium only:
Next (decrease) Row (RS): K1, SSK, work in pattern to last 3 sts, K2 tog, K1.

Next Row (WS): P2, work in pattern to last 2 sts, P2.

Work 2 rows even.

Rep last 4 rows 1{1-0} time(s) more.

For all sizes:
Next (decrease) Row (RS): K1, SSK, work in pattern to last 3 sts, K2 tog, K1.

Next Row (WS): P2, work in pattern to last 2 sts, P2.

Rep these last 2 rows 9{10-15} times more, end with a WS row — 20{21-20} sts.

Top of Cap Shaping: At the beginning of RS rows, bind off 4 sts 3 times, then 5{6-5} sts once AND AT THE SAME TIME, continue to decrease 1 st at the end of the next 3 RS rows.

LEFT SLEEVE
Work same as for Right Sleeve, reversing shaping at top of cap.

FINISHING
Weave Sleeve caps to Fronts and Back along raglan lines *(Fig. 14, page 128)*.

Weave Sleeve and side seams.

Left front trim: With smaller needles and RS facing, pick up 76{78-80} sts evenly along Front edge.

Knit one row.

Bind off in knit.

Right front trim: Work same as for left trim, but make 5-st buttonhole on first WS row, the first at 2 sts down from top neck edge (by binding off 5 sts and casting on 5 sts while working bind off row), and the second 20{22-24} sts below first.

Sew buttons opposite buttonholes.

Collar: With smaller needles, cast on 148{148-166} sts.

Rib rows 1, 5 and 7 (RS): (K2, P2) 4 times, K8, * P2, (K2, P2) 2 times, K8; rep from * across to last 16 sts, end (P2, K2) 4 times.

Rows 2, 4, 6 and 8 (WS): Knit the knit sts and purl the purl sts as they appear.

Row 3 (RS): (K2, P2) 4 times, BC, * P2, (K2, P2) 2 times, BC; rep from * across to last 16 sts, end (P2, K2) 4 times.

Rep Rows 1-8 until collar measures 8" (20.5 cm), end with a WS row.

Shape neckline edge: Bind off 10{10-19} sts at the beginning of the next RS row, then 20 sts at the beginning of the next 2 rows, then 5 sts at the beginning of next 10 rows.

Bind off remaining 48{48-57} sts.

Pin collar to neckline edge with right side of Collar to wrong side of sweater, with initial bind off section along Front neck, and sew firmly in place.

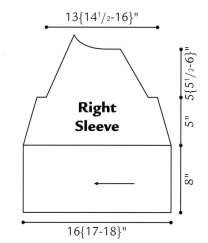

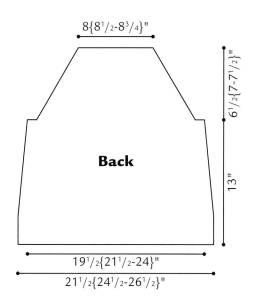

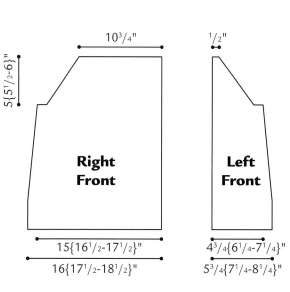

cabled
COMPANIONS

◼◼◼◻ INTERMEDIATE

SIZE: One size fits all
Note: fit can be adjusted on hat band and cuffs

FINISHED MEASUREMENTS
Hat circumference:
approximately 20-23" (51-58.5 cm)
Glove: Fits 7-8" (18-20 cm) hand circumference.

"This allover cable pattern incorporates lace in its lattice structure: it is one of my favorite cable patterns and I have used it in many different ways over the years, in a variety of garments. Here I used it as a panel for the band of the hat and the cuff of the mitts.

"This yarn gives a strong relief, but if you used a softer fiber, like alpaca or a silk blend, the set would have a softer, less crisply-defined quality. I adore the detail of vintage buttons: these stitched leather beauties were bought from a British source."

MATERIALS
BERROCO
"Pure Merino DK"
(100% Wool; 50 grams/
92 yards)
  Color #4523 Baba au Rhum:
  5 balls
Straight knitting needles, size 6
  (4 mm) **or** size to obtain
  given gauge.
Double pointed needles (dpns)
  (set of 5), size 6 (4 mm)
Cable needle (cn)
Stitch markers
Yarn needle
Sewing needle and matching
  thread
$^3/_4$" (19 mm) Buttons - 6

GAUGE
Over Broken Rib:
24 sts and 30 rnds = 4" (10 cm)
Lower Band over 41 sts
should measure 5-5$^1/_4$"
(12.5-13.5 cm) wide.
Take time to save time, check
your gauge.

PATTERN STITCHES
Cable 7 Back (C7B): Slip 4 sts to cn and hold in back, K3 from LH
needle, slip purl st from cn to LH needle and purl it, then K3 from cn.
Cable 7 Front (C7F): Slip 4 sts to cn and hold in front, K3 from LH
needle, slip purl st from cn to LH needle and purl it, then K3 from cn.

CABLE PANEL: Over 35 sts
Row 1 (RS): P1, K1, * YO *(Fig. 3, page 125)*, K2, SSK
(Figs. 11a-c, page 127), P7, K2 tog *(Fig. 8, page 126)*, K2, YO, K1;
rep from * across to last st, end P1.
Row 2: K1, P5, K7, P9, K7, P5, K1.
Row 3: P1, K2, YO, K2, SSK, P5, K2 tog, K2, YO, K2 tog, YO, K1, YO,
K2, SSK, P5, K2 tog, K2, YO, K2, P1.
Row 4: K1, P6, K5, P 11, K5, P6, K1.
Row 5: P1, * K2 tog, YO, K1, YO, K2, SSK, P3, K2 tog, K2, YO,
K2 tog, YO; rep from * across to last 2 sts, K1, P1.
Row 6: K1, P7, K3, P 13, K3, P7, K1.
Row 7: P1, K1, K2 tog, YO, K1, YO, K2, SSK, P1, K2 tog, K2, YO,
(K2 tog, YO) 3 times, K1, YO, K2, SSK, P1, K2 tog, K2, YO, K2 tog,
YO, K2, P1.
Row 8: K1, P8, K1, P 15, K1, P8, K1.
Row 9: P6, C7B, P9, C7B, P6.
Row 10: K6, P3, K1, P3, K9, P3, K1, P3, K6.
Row 11: P5, K2 tog, K2, YO, K1, YO, K2, SSK, P7, K2 tog, K2, YO,
K1, YO, K2, SSK, P5.
Row 12: K5, P9, K7, P9, K5.
Row 13: P4, K2 tog, K2, YO, K2 tog, YO, K1, YO, K2, SSK, P5,
K2 tog, K2, YO, K2 tog, YO, K1, YO, K2, SSK, P4.
Row 14: K4, P 11, K5, P 11, K4.
Row 15: P3, K2 tog, K2, YO, (K2 tog, YO) twice, K1, YO, K2, SSK,
P3, K2 tog, K2, YO, (K2 tog, YO) twice, K1, YO, K2, SSK, P3.
Row 16: K3, P 13, K3, P 13, K3.
Row 17: P2, * K2 tog, K2, YO, (K2 tog, YO) 3 times, K1, YO, K2,
SSK, P1; rep from * across to last st, end P1.
Row 18: K2, (P 15, K1) across to last st, end K1.
Row 19: P2, K3, P9, C7F, P9, K3, P2.
Row 20: K2, P3, K9, P3, K1, P3, K9, P3, K2.
Rep Rows 1-20 for Cable Panel.

CIRCULAR BROKEN RIB: Even number of sts
Rnd 1 (RS): (K1, P1) across.
Rnd 2: Knit.
Rep Rnds 1-2 for Circular Broken Rib.

Note: Keep all edge sts, where noted, in St st.

Instructions begin on page 60.

HAT

Lower band: Cast on 41 sts.

Established Patterns (RS): K3 (edge sts), PM *(see Markers, page 124)*, work Row 1 of Cable Panel over 35 sts, end K3 (edge sts).

Work even as established until band measures 20-23" (51-58.5 cm), or to desired length.

To be sure of fit, wrap band around head with ends meeting to assure a snug, not too tight, fit.

Bind off.

Ribbed flap: With RS facing, pick up 37 sts evenly along cast on edge *(Fig. 13b, page 128)*.

Next Row (WS): P2, K1, (P1, K1) across, end P2.

Next Row (RS): Knit the knit sts, and purl the purl sts as they appear.

Work until edge is ³/₄" (19 mm).

Bind off, decrease 6 sts evenly *(see Decreases, pages 126 & 127 and Decrease Evenly Across A Row, page 126)*, so edge doesn't flare.

Overlap ribbed flap to bound off edge of band, then try on to check fit again.

Sew in place underneath flap, so that picked-up flap sts on WS meet bound-off edge of lower band.

Crown of hat:

Place markers to divide one side of the hat band into 4 sections *(see Double Pointed Needles, page 125)*.

With RS facing, picking up into the inside of the band, along the edge that is next to the edge sts, pick up 30 sts in each section, each with a separate dpn —120 sts.

Place marker for beginning of rnd and join.

With a 5th dpn, work 2 rnds of Broken Rib over all 4 needles.

Next (decrease) rnd: Work in pattern to last 2 sts of dpn, K2 tog; rep on remaining 3 needles.

Rep decrease rnd EVERY rnd until there are 4 sts remaining.

Placing 4 sts on one dpn, cast on 6 sts — 10 sts.

Knit 1 row, purl 1 row.

Bind off in knit.

Tack this tab down at top of Hat.

FINISHING

Sew 2 buttons to flap of hat band, through all layers.

FINGERLESS GLOVES

Cuffs (make 2): Cast on 41 sts.

Next Row (RS): K3 (edge sts), place marker (PM) *(see Markers, page 124)*, work Row 1 of Cable Panel over 35 sts, end K3 (edge sts).

Work even as established until band measures 7" (18 cm) [for larger arm, work to 7¹/₂-8" (19-20.5) if desired].

Bind off.

LEFT GLOVE

Ribbed flap: With RS facing, pick up 37 sts evenly along cast on edge *(Fig. 13b, page 128)*.

Next Row (WS): P2, K1, (P1, K1) across, end P2.

Next Row (RS): Knit the knit sts, and purl the purl sts as they appear.

Work until edge is ³/₄" (19 mm).

Bind off, decrease 6 sts evenly *(see Decreases, pages 126 & 127 and Decrease Evenly Across A Row, page 126)*, so edge doesn't flare.

Overlap ribbed flap to bound off edge of band.

Sew in place underneath flap, so that picked-up flap sts on WS meet bound-off edge of cuff.

Hand: With RS facing, dpns and beginning at the left edge of the ribbed flap, pick up 44 sts evenly along one edge of cuff and distribute over 4 needles. Place marker and join.

Work in Broken Rib until section measures approximately $^3/_4$" (19 mm), end with a knit rnd.

Established Gusset:
Next rnd (make outline sts): Work 20 sts, PM, K1 (outline st #1), M1-p (outline st #2), PM, work as established to end — 45 sts.

Keeping outline sts in St st, work even for 1 more rnd.

Next (established gusset st) rnd: Work to marker, slip marker, K1 (1st outline st), M1-p (thumb gusset), knit 2nd outline st, slip marker, work to end — 46 sts.

Keeping outline sts in St st, and center st in pattern, work even for 3 more rnds.

Next (double increase gusset) rnd: Work as established, making a new st in pattern AFTER first outline st, and BEFORE 2nd outline st, working all other sts in pattern as established — 48 sts (3 gusset sts in pattern between outline sts).

Keeping to patterns as established, rep double increase gusset rnd every 4th rnd 6 times more — 60 sts (there are 15 gusset sts between outline sts).

Work 1 rnd even.

Next rnd: Work 21 sts (includes first outline st), then cast on 4 sts, slip next 16 sts to yarn holder, work remaining 23 sts to end — 48 sts.

Work in Broken Rib over all 48 sts as established until section above cast-on measures $1^3/_4$-2" (4.5-5 cm), end with Rnd 1.

Bind off.

Thumb: Slip 16 sts to dpns.

Work 16 sts in pattern as established, then pick up 4 sts in cast on sts of hand — 20 sts.

Distribute evenly over 4 needles. Place marker and join.

Work in Broken Rib as established until thumb measures $1^1/_4$-$1^3/_8$" (3-3.5 cm), end with Rnd 1.

Bind off.

RIGHT GLOVE
Work same as for Left Glove, reversing patterns and gusset as follows:
Pick up 37 flap sts on bound off edge of Cuff and when completed, sew to cast-on edge.

Reverse placement of gusset by picking up hand sts beginning at the right edge of flap.

FINISHING
Sew 2 buttons to flap of both gloves, through all layers.

carefree
CABLES

◖■◻◻ **EASY**

SIZES
To fit sizes Small{Medium-Large-Extra Large}.
Sample in size Small.

FINISHED MEASUREMENTS
Bust at underarm:
$36^1/_2${$40^1/_2$-$44^1/_2$-$48^1/_2$}"/92.5{103-113-123} cm
Length to back neck:
25{$25^1/_2$-26-$26^1/_2$}"/63.5{65-66-67.5} cm

Size Note: Instructions are written for size Small with sizes Medium, Large, and Extra Large in braces { }. Instructions will be easier to read if you circle all the numbers pertaining to your size. If only one number is given, it applies to all sizes.

"I love garter stitch—just knit every row! And in this sweater I added a few twists. I easily elongated some rows by using a larger needle—this accents the yoke and decorates the simple cable. An easy to wear piece to have on hand every day of 'sweater season'.

"I chose this specially dyed yarn to perk up the simplicity of the sweater, and added the lace eyelets at the side seams for detail too."

MATERIALS

QUEENSLAND COLLECTION
"Rustic Tweed" **MEDIUM 4**
(63% Wool, 27% Alpaca, 10% Donegal;
100 grams/278 yards)
Color #906 (Salmon):
5{5-6-7} hanks
Straight knitting needles, sizes 10 (6 mm) **and** 15 (10 mm) **or** size to obtain gauge
24" (61 cm) Circular knitting needle size 10 (6 mm)
Cable needle (cn)
Stitch markers
Yarn needle

GAUGE

Garter St using size 10 needles:
16 sts and 32 rows = 4" (10 cm)
Cable worked over 10 sts measures approximately $1^3/4$" (4.5 cm) wide
Take time to save time, check your gauge.

PATTERN STITCHES

GARTER STITCH: Any number of sts
Knit every row.

Note: Garter St sections of the sweater will be knit every row, EXCEPT when WS Row 10 of Cable is being worked, that row will be purled across entire row.

CABLE: Over 10 sts
Rows 1, 3 (RS): With size 10 needles, K 10.
Rows 2, 4, 6 and 8: P 10.
Row 5: Slip 5 sts to cn and hold in back, K5 from LH needle, then K5 from cn.
Row 7: K 10.
Row 9: Change to size 15 needles, K 10.
Row 10: With size 15 needles, P 10 (see note).
Rows 11 and 13: Change to size 10 needles, K 10.
Rows 12 and 14: P 10.
Rep Rows 1-14 for Cable.

Instructions begin on page 66.

BACK

Note: Slip the first st of every row with yarn in back (wyib).

With size 10 needles, cast on 88{96-104-112} sts.

Row 1 (RS): Slip 1 wyib, K2, YO *(Fig. 3, page 125)*, K2 tog *(Fig. 8, page 126)*, knit across to last 5 sts, SSK *(Figs. 11a-c, page 127)*, YO, K3.

Rows 2, 3 and 4: Slip 1 wyib, knit across.

Rep the last 4 rows until piece measures 12" (30.5 cm), end with a WS row.

Established Cabled Section (and decrease) (RS): Keeping edge eyelets as established, decrease 6 sts as follows: Work 14{18-22-26} sts, K2 tog, PM *(see Markers, page 124)*, work Row 1 of Cable over next 10 sts, PM, K2 tog, K9, K2 tog, PM, work Row 1 of Cable over next 10 sts, PM, K2 tog, K9, K2 tog, PM, work Row 1 of Cable over next 10 sts, PM, K2 tog, work remaining 14{18-22-26} sts — 82{90-98-106} sts.

Next Row (WS): Work 15{19-23-27} sts, slip marker, (work Row 2 of Cable over 10 sts, slip marker, K 11, slip marker) twice, work Row 2 of Cable over 10 sts, slip marker, work remaining K 15{19-23-27} sts.

Work even as established until Row 8 of Cable is complete.

Change to size 15 needles.

Work Elongated band (RS): Work to marker, slip marker, (work Row 9 of Cable over 10 sts, slip marker, K 11, slip marker) twice, work Row 9 of Cable over 10 sts, slip marker, work to end.

Next Row (WS): Purl across. (see note on page 64)

Change back to size 10 needles, and resume Patterns as established, changing to size 15 needles for rows 9 and 10 of cable AND AT THE SAME TIME, do not work an eyelet at edges of row following elongated rows, but instead K2 rows before resuming eyelets at beginning and end of every 4th row.

Work until piece measures 17¹/₂" (44.5 cm), end with a WS row.

Note: Discontinue eyelets at beginning and end of rows.

Armhole Shaping: Bind off 4 sts at the beginning of the next 2 rows — 74{82-90-98} sts.

Next (decrease) Row (RS): Slip 1 wyib, K1, SSK, work to last 4 sts, K2 tog, K2 — 72{80-88-96} sts.

Working in patterns as established, rep decrease row every 4th row 3{5-7-9} times more — 66{70-74-78} sts.

Work even until armhole measures 6¹/₂{7-7¹/₂-8}"/ 16.5{18-19-20.5} cm, end with a WS row.

Discontinue elongated rows and work with size 10 needles only.

Back Neck Shaping: Mark center 20 sts.

Next Row (RS): Work to marked sts, join a second ball of yarn and bind off center 20 sts, work to end.

Keeping in pattern, working both sides with separate balls of yarn, bind off from each neck edge 4 sts 4 times AND AT THE SAME TIME, when armhole measures 7¹/₂{8-8¹/₂-9}"/ 19{20.5-21.5-23} cm, end with a WS row — 7{9-11-13} sts each side.

Shoulder Shaping: Bind off 2{3-4-4} sts at beginning of next 4 rows, then 3{3-3-5} sts at beginning of next 2 rows.

FRONT

Work as for Back until armhole measures 6{6¹/₂-7-7¹/₂}"/ {15-18-19} cm, end with a WS row.

Front neck shaping: Mark center 20 sts.

Next Row (RS): Work to marked sts, join a second ball of yarn and bind off center 20 sts, work to end.

Keeping in pattern, working both sides with separate balls of yarn, bind off from each neck edge 4 sts 4 times AND AT THE SAME TIME, when armhole measures 7¹/₂{8-8¹/₂-9}"/ 19{20.5-21.5-23} cm, end with a WS row.

Shoulder Shaping: Bind off 2{3-4-4} sts at beginning of next 4 rows, then 3{3-3-5} sts at beginning of next 2 rows. — 7{9-11-13} sts.

SLEEVE

Note: Slip the first st of every row wyib.

With size 10 needles, cast on 57{61-65-69} sts.

Row 1 (RS): slip 1 wyib, K2, YO, K2 tog, knit across to last 5 sts, SSK, YO, K3.

Rows 2, 3 and 4: Slip 1 wyib, knit across to end.

Rep the last 4 rows until piece measures 12" (30.5 cm), end with a WS row.

Established Cabled Section (and decrease) (RS): Keeping edge eyelets as established, decrease 3 sts as follows: work 21{23-25-27} sts, K2 tog, PM, K5, K2 tog, K4, PM, K2 tog, work remaining 21{23-25-27} sts — 54{58-62-66} sts.

Next Row (WS): Work 22{24-26-28} sts, slip marker, work Row 2 of Cable over center 10 sts, slip marker, work remaining 22{24-26-28} sts.

Work until Row 8 of Cable is complete.

Change to size 15 needles.

Work elongated band (RS): Work 22{24-26-28}, slip marker, work Row 9 of Cable over 10 sts, slip marker, work remaining 22{24-26-28} sts.

Next Row (WS): Purl all sts. (see note on page 64)

Change back to size 10 needles, and resume Patterns as established, changing to size 15 needles for rows 9 and 10 of cable AND AT THE SAME TIME, do not work an eyelet at edges of row following an elongated row, but instead knit 2 rows before resuming eyelets at beginning and end of every 4th row.

Work as established until piece measures 17¹/₂" (44.5 cm), end with a WS row.

Note: Discontinue eyelets at beginning and end of row.

Cap Shaping (RS): Bind off 4 sts at the beginning of the next 2 rows — 46{50-54-58} sts.

Next (decrease) Row (RS): Slip 1 wyib, K1, SSK, work to last 4 sts, K2 tog, K2 — 44{48-52-56} sts.

Rep decrease row every RS row 11{13-15-17} more times — 22 sts.

Bind off 2 sts at the beginning of the next 2 rows.

Bind off remaining 18 sts.

FINISHING

Sew Front to Back at shoulder.

Weave side seams and Sleeve seams *(Fig. 14, page 128)*.

Sew Sleeve caps into armholes.

Neck finishing: With circular needle and RS facing, pick up 98 sts evenly around neckline *(Figs. 13a & b, page 128)*; place marker and join.

Knit 1 rnd.

Bind off purlwise.

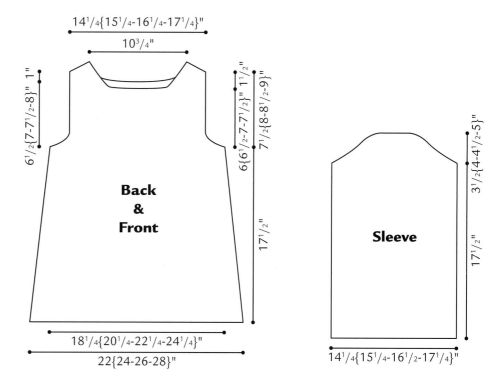

cosmopolitan
CABLES

◖◼◼◼▢ INTERMEDIATE

SIZES
To fit Small{Medium-Large-Extra Large}.
Sample in size Small.

FINISHED MEASUREMENTS
Bust at underarm:
38{42-46-49}"/96.5{106.5-117-124.5} cm
Length from outer shoulder:
$25^1/_2${26-26$^1/_2$-27}"/65{66-67.5-68.5} cm

Size Note: Instructions are written for size Small with sizes Medium, Large, and Extra Large in braces { }. Instructions will be easier to read if you circle all the numbers pertaining to your size. If only one number is given, it applies to all sizes.

"To 'move' a cable on the diagonal across a knitted fabric is fun! It is easy to do: over a number of rows you decrease on one side of the cable and increase on the other side, then the cabled slants over the surface of the fabric. In this sweater, I moved the central cables in opposite directions to form a V-shaped yoke filled in with my favorite textured pattern, seed stitch.

"This design has an easy knit-in collar that grows out of the body of the sweater. The smooth cables contrast well with the simple checked and seeded textures. A bouncy yarn helps to make the texture 'pop'!

"The choice of wool, a naturally spring fiber, keep the dense quality of the ribbing for a close fit. This sweater would be less fitted in a yarn that was less springy—an alpaca or cotton yarn."

MATERIALS

CLASSIC ELITE [BULKY 5]

"Montera"

(50% Llama, 50% Wool;
100 grams/127 yards)
  Color #3862 (Kingfisher
  Blue):
  10{11-12-14} hanks
Straight knitting needles, size 9
  (5.5 mm) **or** size needed to
  obtain gauge
24" (61 cm) Circular knitting
  needle, size 9 (5.5 mm)
Cable needle (cn)
Stitch markers
Stitch holders - 2
Yarn needle

GAUGE

Double Moss St:
15 sts and 26 rows = 4" (10 cm)
Seed St:
15 sts and 28 rows = 4" (10 cm)
K2, P2 Rib:
18 sts and 20 rows = 4" (10 cm)
18 st Cable Panel:
approximately 2^1/$_2$" (6.5 cm) wide
Take time to save time, check your
gauge.

PATTERN STITICHES

Back Cross (BC): Slip 3 sts to cn and hold in back, K3 from
LH needle, K3 from cn.

Front Cross (FC): Slip 3 sts to cn and hold in front, K3 from
LH needle, K3 from cn.

STOCKINETTE STITCH (St st): Any number of sts
Knit RS rows, purl WS rows.

SEED ST: Odd number of sts
All rows: P1, (K1, P1) across.

K2, P2 RIB: Multiple of 4 sts plus 2
Row 1 (RS): K2, (P2, K2) across.
Row 2: P2, (K2, P2) across.
Rep Rows 1 and 2 for K2, P2 Rib.

DOUBLE MOSS ST: Multiple of 4 sts plus 2
Row 1 (RS): P2, (K2, P2) across.
Row 2: K2, (P2, K2) across.
Row 3: K2, (P2, K2) across.
Row 4: P2, (K2, P2) across.
Rep Rows 1-4 for Double Moss St.

CABLE PANEL: Over 18 sts
Rows 1 and 3 (RS): P2, (K6, P2) twice.
Row 2 and all WS rows: K2, (P6, K2) twice.
Row 5: P2, BC, P2, FC, P2.
Row 7: P2, (K6, P2) twice.
Row 8: K2, (P6, K2) twice.
Rep Rows 1-8 for Cable Panel.

Note: Keep all edge sts, where noted, in St st.

Instructions begin on page 72.

BACK

Cast on 94{102-110-118} sts.

Established Patterns (RS):
Work in K2, P2 Rib over 38{42-46-50} sts, PM **(see Markers, page 124)**, work Cable Panel over center 18 sts, PM, work in K2, P2 Rib over remaining 38{42-46-50} sts.

Work even in patterns as established until piece measures 14" (35.5 cm), end with a RS row.

Next (decrease) Row (WS):
Work rib as established over 38{42-46-50} sts and decrease 6 sts evenly spaced **(see Decreases, pages 126 & 127 and Decreasing Evenly Across A Row, page 126)**, slip marker, continue Cable Panel as established over center 18 sts, slip marker, work in rib over remaining 38{42-46-50} sts and decrease 6 sts evenly spaced — 82{90-98-106} sts.

Established Patterns (RS):
K2 (edges sts), work in Double Moss St over 30{34-38-42} sts, slip marker, continue Cable Panel as established over center 18 sts, slip marker, work in Double Moss St over 30{34-38-42} sts, K2 (edges sts).

Work in patterns as established until piece measures 18" (45.5 cm), end with a WS row.

Armhole Shaping: Bind off 4 sts at the beginning of the next 2 rows — 74{82-90-98} sts.

Next (decrease) Row (RS): K1, SSK **(Figs. 11a-c, page 127)**, work across to last 3 sts, K2 tog **(Fig 8, page 126)**, K1.

Keeping 2 sts each side in St st for edge sts, rep decrease row every RS row 4{6-8-10} times more — 64{68-72-76} sts.

Discontinue edge sts above armhole shaping and work them in Double Moss st.

Work even until armhole measures $7^1/_2${$8-8^1/_2$-9}"/ 19{20.5-21.5-23} cm, end with a WS row.

Shoulder Shaping: Bind off 5{5-5-7} sts at beginning of next 2 rows, then 4{5-6-6} sts at beginning of next 4 rows.

Slip remaining 38 sts to st holder.

FRONT

Work as for Back until piece measures $16^3/_4$" (42.5 cm), end with Row 1, 5 or 7.

Next (increase) Row (WS): P2 (edge sts), work as established in Double Moss St over 30{34-38-42} sts, slip marker, K2, P6, M1 **(Figs. 6a & b, page 126)**, K2, M1, P6, K2, slip marker, work as established in Double Moss St over 30{34-38-42} sts, end P2 (edge sts) — 84{92-100-108} sts.

Mark Center st (RS): Work as established to marker, slip marker, P2, K6, P2, PM, M1 (mark this center st), PM, P2, K6, P2, slip marker, work as established to end — 85{93-101-109} sts.

Next Row (WS): Work to marker, slip marker, K2, P6, K2 (continue individual cable as established over these 10 sts), slip marker, K center st, slip marker, then P2, K6, P2 (continue individual cable as established over these 10 sts), slip marker, work to end.

Remove outermost markers, keep markers at center.

Cable moving Row (RS): Work as established to 1 st before cable panel, P2 tog (the last st of Double Moss section with first purl st of Cable Panel) **(Fig. 9, page 127)**, work remaining 9 sts of Cable Panel as established, slip marker, M1, K center st (Seed st), M1, slip marker, work 9 sts of Cable Panel as established, P2 tog [the last purl st of Cable Panel tog with first st of Double Moss section], work as established to end.

Next Row (WS): Work as established, keeping 10 sts in each Cable section, and work Seed st in center 3 sts (note that there is one less st in Double Moss Pattern on each side).

Work 2 rows even.

Working center increases into Seed St, rep Cable moving row on next row, then alternately every 2nd and 4th rows for a total of 16{17-18-19} increases each side of center st, [there are 33{35-37-39} sts in Seed St at center] AND AT THE SAME TIME, when piece measures same as Back to armhole, work armhole shaping as for Back — 67{71-75-79} sts.

Work even until armhole measures same as Back to shoulder, end with a WS row.

Shoulder Shaping (RS): Bind off 5{5-5-7} sts at beginning of next 2 rows, then 4{5-6-6} sts at beginning of next 4 rows.

Slip remaining 41 sts to st holder.

SLEEVES
Cast on 54{58-62-66} sts.

Work in K2, P2 Rib until Sleeve measures 14" (35.5 cm), end with a WS row.

Established Patterns (RS): K2 (edge sts), work Row 1 of Double Moss St over center 50{54-58-62} sts, end K2 (edge sts).

Work in patterns as established until Sleeve measures 18" (45.5 cm), end with a WS row.

Cap Shaping: Bind off 4 sts at the beginning of the next 2 rows — 46{50-54-58} sts.

Next (decrease) Row (RS): K1, SSK, knit across to last 3 sts, K2 tog, K1.

Keeping 2 sts each side in St st for edge sts, rep decrease row every RS row 11{12-14-16} times more — 22{24-24-24} sts.

Bind off 2 sts at the beginning of the next 4{2-2-2} rows, then 3 sts at beginning of next 0{2-2-2} rows **(see Zeros, page 124)**.

Bind off remaining 14 sts.

FINISHING
Sew Front to Back at shoulder.

Weave side seams **(Fig. 14, page 128)**.

Collar: With RS facing, beginning at right shoulder seam, slip 38 Back sts to circular needle, PM at left shoulder seam, then slip 41 Front sts to circular needle —79 sts; place marker at right shoulder and join.

Next rnd (RS of sweater facing, WS of collar facing): P1, work in Seed st as established over Back neck sts to 1 st before marker, P1, slip marker, P1, work in Seed st as established over Front neck sts to 1 st before marker, P1, slip marker.

Purl sts before and after markers and keeping collar sts in Seed St as established, work even for 6 rnds.

Next (increase) rnd: * P1, M1, work to 1 st before marker, M1, P1, slip marker; rep from * across.

Working increases into Seed st, work even for 5 more rnds, then rep increase rnd on next rnd, then every 6th rnd until collar measures 10" (25.5 cm).

Bind off in Seed St.

Weave Sleeve seams.

Sew Sleeve caps into armholes.

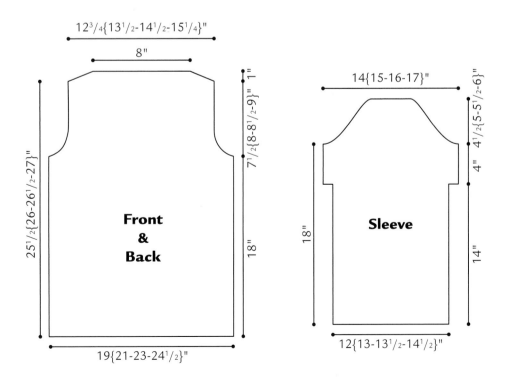

cabled
CARRY-ALL

◖■■▭ INTERMEDIATE

FINISHED MEASUREMENTS
Width, not including side panel: 15" (38 cm)
Height, not including strap: 14$^1/_2$" (37 cm)

"This fun-to-knit bag works in any season, depending on what yarn you choose! Here there is a version for winter in a dyed wool, and one for summer in a crisp cotton blend. Finding a beautiful buckle to complement the bag is part of the fun!

"I planned the bag to incorporate a wide cable, with lots of texture. Some easy shaping gives the bag its unique profile. A small easy-to-knit twist-stitch cable on each side of the lower panel helps make a neat "fold" where the band meets the main section of the bag. These small cables extend up into and lend body to the wide handle section. Easy to wear and capacious too! If firmly knit, there is no need to line this bag."

MATERIALS

OPTION ONE

BLUE SKY WORSTED
"Hand Dyes"
(50% Alpaca, 50% Merino
Wool;
100 grams/109 yards)
Color #2004 (Purple):
7 hanks

OPTION TWO

SCHULANA
"Supercotton"
(70% Cotton, 30% Polyester;
50 grams/98 yards)
Color #30 (Turquoise):
9 skeins
Straight knitting needles, size 9
(5.5 mm) **or** size to obtain
given gauge
Cable needle (cn)
Stitch markers
Yarn needle
Large Buckle
$3/4$" (18 mm) Snap magnetic

GAUGE

Over St St with size 9 needles:
16 sts and 24 rows = 4" (10 cm)
Over Textured Rib Pattern with size 9
needles:
19 sts and 23 rows = 4" (10 cm)
Wide Cable over 30 sts
measures appox. $5^{1}/_2$" (14 cm) wide.
Take time to save time, check your
gauge.

PATTERN STITCHES

Back Cross (BC): Slip 2 sts to cn and hold in back, K2 from LH needle, K2 from cn.

Front Cross (FC): Slip 2 sts to cn and hold in front, K2 from LH needle, K2 from cn.

Twist 3 Front (T3F): Slip 2 sts to cn and hold in front, P1 from LH needle, K2 from cn.

Twist 3 Back (T3B): Slip 1 st to cn and hold in back, K2 from LH needle, P1 from cn.

Cluster 4 (worked from the WS): Slip 4 wyib, pass yarn to front, slip the same 4 sts back to LH needle, pass yarn to back, slip 4 wyib again.

STOCKINETTE STITCH (St st): Any number of sts
Knit RS rows, purl WS rows.

TEXTURED RIB: Multiple of 5 sts plus 1
Row 1 (RS): K tbl *(Fig. 4, page 125)*, (P1, K2, P1, K tbl) across.
Row 2: P1, (K1, P2, K1, P1) across.
Row 3: K tbl, (P4, K tbl) across.
Row 4: P1, (K4, P1) across.
Rep Rows 1-4 for Textured Rib.

WIDE CABLE: Over 30 sts
Row 1 (RS): P3, FC, BC, P8, FC, BC, P3.
Rows 2 and 4: K3, P8, K8, P8, K3.
Row 3: P3, K8, P8, K8, P3.
Rows 5-9: Rep Rows 1-4, then Row 1 again.
Row 10: K3, P2, Cluster 4, P2, K8, P2, Cluster 4, P2, K3.
Row 11: P2, T3B, P4, T3F, P6, T3B, P4, T3F, P2.
Row 12: K2, P2, (K6, P2) 3 times, K2.
Row 13: P1, T3B, P6, T3F, P4, T3B, P6, T3F, P1.
Row 14: K1, P2, K8, P2, Cluster 4, P2, K8, P2, K1.

Row 15: P1, K2, P8, FC, BC, P8, K2, P1.
Rows 16 and 18: K1, P2, K8, P8, K8, P2, K1.
Row 17: P1, K2, P8, K8, P8, K2, P1.
Rows 19-23: Rep Rows 15-18; then Row 15 again.
Row 24: K1, P2, K8, P2, Cluster 4, P2, K8, P2, K1.
Row 25: P1, T3F, P6, T3B, P4, T3F, P6, T3B, P1.
Row 26: K2, P2, (K6, P2) 3 times, K2.
Row 27: P2, T3F, P4, T3B, P6, T3F, P4, T3B, P2.
Row 28: K3, P2, Cluster 4, P2, K8, P2, Cluster 4, P2, K3.
Rep Rows 1-28.

TWISTED RIB CABLE: Over 8 sts
Rows 1 and 3 (WS): K2, P4, K2.
Row 2: P2, [K2 tog *(Fig. 8, page 126)* but do not slip st from needle; insert right-hand needle between the sts just knitted together, and knit the first st again; then slip both sts from needle tog] twice, P2.
Row 4: P2, K1, K2 tog and knit first st again as before; K1, P2.
Rep Rows 1-4 for Twisted Rib Cable.

Right leaning decrease: Slip 1 st on cn and hold in back, slip next st through back loop, knit tog with st from cn.
Left leaning decrease: Slip 1 through back loop, slip next through front loop, K2 tog.

Note: Work all edge sts, where noted, in St St.

Instructions begin on page 78.

FRONT

Cast on 76 sts.

Established Patterns (RS):
K2 (edge sts), work Row 1 of Textured Rib over 21 sts, PM *(see Markers, page 124)*, work Row 1 of Wide cable over 30 sts, PM, work Row 1 of Textured Rib over 21 sts, end K2 (edge sts).

Work as established until piece measures 6" (15 cm), end with Row 4 of Wide cable.

Next (decrease) Row (RS):
Work to last 2 sts of Textured Rib, work 1 right leaning decrease, slip marker, work Cable panel, slip marker, work 1 left leaning decrease, work to end.

Keeping in pattern, rep decrease row every 4th row 9 times more — 56 sts.

Work even until Row 14 of pattern is complete.

Curve top: Mark center 32 sts.

Work 12 sts, join a second ball of yarn and bind off center 32 sts, work to end — 12 sts each side.

Working both sides at once, bind off 2 sts each side of inner edge 6 times.

BACK

Work same as for Front.

BOTTOM CENTER CABLE PANEL

Cast on 10 sts.

Row 1 and all WS rows: K1, P8, K1.

Row 2 (RS): P1, BC, FC, P1.

Row 4: P1, K8, P1.

Rep Rows 1-4 until piece measures approximately 5½" (14 cm), end with a RS Row 2.

Bind off on WS row.

RIGHT HAND BOTTOM AND SIDE PANEL

With RS of Cable Strip facing, pick up 36 sts evenly along one side *(Fig. 13a, page 128)*.

Established Patterns (WS):
P2 (edge sts), PM, work Row 1 of Twisted Rib Cable over 8 sts, PM, work Row 2 of Textured Rib over center 16 sts, PM, work Row 1 of Twisted Rib Cable over 8 sts, PM, end P2 (edge sts).

Next Row (RS): K1, K tbl (edge sts), slip marker, work Row 2 of Twisted Rib Cable over 8 sts, slip marker, work Row 1 of Textured Rib over center 16 sts, slip marker, work Row 2 of Twisted Rib Cable over 8 sts, slip marker, end K tbl, K1 (edge sts).

Working in patterns as established, until piece measures 7" (18 cm) from picked up edge, then tie yarn markers at each end.

Continue in patterns as established until piece measures 5" (12.5 cm) from yarn markers, end with a WS row.

Next (decrease) Row (RS):
Work to Textured Rib, slip marker, work 1 right leaning decrease, work to last 2 sts of Textured Rib, work 1 left leaning decrease, work to end.

Rep decrease row every 8th row 4 times more — 26 sts.

Work even until piece, from yarn marker, measures same as side of bag, end with a WS row.

Slip sts to holder.

LEFT HAND BOTTOM, SIDE PANEL AND HANDLE

Work same as for Right hand bottom and side, but place 2nd yarn marker on each side when piece measures same as side bag.

Continue on all sts until strap section, beyond 2nd marker measures 26" (66 cm), end with a WS row.

Slip sts to st holder.

FINISHING

Trim for top of bag: With RS facing, pick up 44 sts evenly along entire bound-off curved upper edge.

Knit 1 row, purl 1 row.

Bind off loosely on WS.

Rep for top of back piece.

Ribbed strap: Slip sts from shorter end of side panel to needle with RS facing.

Next Row (RS): K2 tog *(Fig. 8, page 126)*, * P2 tog *(Fig. 9, page 127)*, K2 tog; rep from * across — 13 sts.

Next Row (WS): (P1, K1) to last st, P1.

Work in K1, P1 Rib as established for 3" (7.5 cm).

Bind off.

Slide ribbed band through center of buckle, fold in half and sew in place at base of ribbing.

Rep ribbed strap on other end until piece measures 3" (7.5 cm), end with a WS row.

SHAPE POINT

Next Row (RS) SSK, rib to last 2 sts, K2 tog.

Next Row (WS): P1, rib to last st, P1.

Rep last 2 rows until 3 sts remain.

Weave end to WS.

Weave bottom and side panels to Front and Back, centering bottom cable panel *(Fig. 14, page 128)*.

Sew snap at inside center if desired.

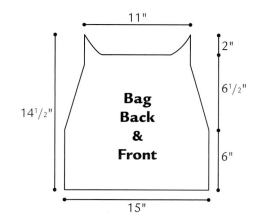

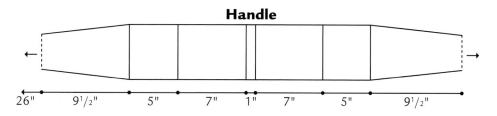

classic
CABLES

◖◼◼◻ INTERMEDIATE

SIZE
To fit sizes Small{Medium-Large-ExtraLarge}.
Sample in size Small.

FINISHED MEASUREMENTS
Bust at underarm: 36{40-44-48}"/91.5{101.5-112-122} cm
Length from back neck: $24^3/_4${$25^1/_4$-$25^3/_4$-$26^1/_4$}"/63{64-65.5-66.5} cm

Size Note: Instructions are written for size Small with sizes Medium, Large, and Extra Large in braces { }. Instructions will be easier to read if you circle all the numbers pertaining to your size. If only one number is given, it applies to all sizes.

"This simple cable pattern, bands of texture and cables, works nicely in this cotton blend yarn that has a little glitter. I am fond of sweaters with raglan shaping—they fit well and are comfortable to wear.

"To vary this design you might work the cabled bands in stripes of color. If you used a warmer fiber, or a firm cotton or linen, this dressy evening sweater could be transformed into a more everyday garment."

MATERIALS
LOUISA HARDING  `[LIGHT 3]`
"Jasmine"
(48% Alpaca, 39% Bamboo,
    10% Silk, 3% Polyester;
    50 grams/107 yards)
Color #1 (Ivory):
    11{13-14-15} skeins
Straight knitting needles sizes,
    5 (3.75 mm) **and** 6 (4 mm)
    or size needed to obtain
    gauge
24" (61 cm) Circular knitting
    needle, size 5 (3.75 mm)
Cable needle (cn)
Stitch markers
Yarn needle

GAUGE
Garter and Rev St st using
larger needles:
23 sts and 32 rows = 4" (10 cm)
Cable Pattern rows 1-6 using
larger needles:
23 sts and 32 rows = 4" (10 cm)
Cable Pattern rows 7-18 using
larger needles:
27 sts and 32 rows = 4" (10 cm)
Take time to save time, check
your gauge.

PATTERN STITCHES
Back Cross (BC): Slip 3 sts to cn and hold in back, K3 from LH needle, K3 from cn.
Right Twist (RT): K2 tog *(Fig. 8, page 126)*, do not slip sts from needle, insert RH needle between sts just worked and knit first st again, slip both sts from needle.

STOCKINETTE STITCH (St st): Any number of sts
Knit on RS, purl on WS.

GARTER AND REVERSE STOCKINETTE STITCH:
Any number of sts
Rows 1-6: Knit across.
Row 7 (RS): Knit across.
Rows 8 (WS): Purl across.
Rows 9, 11, 13, 15, 17 (RS): Purl across.
Rows 10, 12, 14, 16 (WS): Knit across.
Row 18 (WS): Purl across.
Rep Rows 1-18 for Garter and Rev St st.

CABLE PATTERN
Begins as a Multiple of 10 sts
Note: Stitch count varies from row to row. Rows 1 to 6 are a Multiple of 10 sts, Rows 7 to 18 (cabled section) are a Multiple of 12 sts.
Rows 1-6: Knit across.
Row 7 (RS): * K5, M1 *(Figs. 6a & b, page 126)*; rep from * across.
Row 8 (WS): Purl across.
Rows 9 and 11 (RS): P3, K6, (P6, K6) across to last 3 sts, end P3.
Rows 10 and 12 (WS): K3, (P6, K6) across to last 9 sts, end P6, K3.
Row 13 (RS): P3, BC, (P6, BC) across to last 3 sts, end P3.
Row 14 and 16 (WS): Same as Row 10.
Row 15 and 17 (RS): Same as Row 9.
Row 18 (WS): P2 tog *(Fig. 9, page 127)*, P3, P2 tog, (P4, P2 tog) across to last 5 sts, P5.
Rep Rows 1-18 for Cable Pattern.

Note: All st counts are based on number of sts on pattern Rows 1-6 of center Cable Pattern.

Instructions begin on page 84.

BACK

With smaller needles, cast on 104{116-128-138} sts.

Knit 1 RS row, purl 1 WS row.

Change to larger needles.

Next Row (RS): Work 22{23-24-24} sts in Garter and Rev St st, PM (see Markers), work center 60{70-80-90} sts in Cable Pattern, PM, work 22{23-24-24} sts in Garter and Rev St st.

Work even in patterns as established for 7 more rows, end with a WS row.

Next (decrease) Row (RS): K2, SSK *(Figs. 11a-c, page 127)*, work as established to last 4 sts, K2 tog *(Fig. 8, page 126)*, K2.

Keeping in pattern as established, rep decrease every 8th row 5 times more — 92{104-116-126} sts (if on rows 1-6 of center pattern st) or 104{118-132-144} sts (if on rows 7-18 of center pattern st).

Work even until piece measures 9" (23 cm), end with a WS row.

Next (increase) row (RS): K2, M1, work as established to last 2 sts, M1, K2.

Keeping in pattern as established, rep increase row every 8th row 5 times more — 104{116-128-138} sts.

Work even until piece measures 17" (43 cm), ending on Row 14 of patterns.

Note: While working raglan decreases into center Cable Pattern, if st and row counts prevent an entire cable to be worked at each side, do not do increases and decreases associated with that cable and work sts in St st instead. Remember this when counting final sts.

Raglan armhole shaping:
Keeping in patterns, bind off 6 sts at the beginning of the next 2 rows, then 2 sts at the beginning of the next 2 rows.

Next (decrease) Row (RS): K2, SSK, work to last 4 sts, K2 tog, K2.

Keeping 2 sts each side in St st for edges and continue in patterns as established, rep decrease row every 4th row 5{4-3-2} times more, then every 2nd row 9{13-17-21} times.

Bind off remaining 58{64-70-74} sts. (Remember, st counts vary depending on which pattern row you are on.)

FRONT

Work same as for Back.

SLEEVE

With smaller needles, cast on 48{52-54-54} sts.

Knit 1 RS row, purl 1 WS row.

Change to larger needles.

Knit 4 rows.

Next Row (RS): Work 4{6-7-7} sts in Garter and Rev St st, PM, work center 40 sts in Cable Pattern, PM, work 4{6-7-7} sts in Garter and Rev St st.

Work even in patterns for 3" (7.5 cm), end with a WS row.

Next (increase) Row (RS): K2, M1, work as established to last 2 sts, M1, K2.

Keeping in pattern as established, rep increase row every 4th row 0{0-0-3} times *(see Zeros, page 124)*, every 6th row 0{2-10-16} times, then every 8th row 13{12-6-0} times — 76{82-88-94} sts.

Work even until piece measures 18" (45.5 cm), ending on Row 14 of patterns.

Note: While working raglan decreases into center Cable Pattern, if st and row counts prevent an entire cable to be worked at each side, do not do increases and decreases associated with that cable, and work sts in St st instead. Remember this when counting final sts.

Raglan Cap Shaping: Keeping in patterns, bind off 6 sts at the beginning of the next 2 rows, then 2 sts at the beginning of the next 2 rows.

Next (decrease) Row (RS): K2, SSK, work across to last 4 sts, K2 tog, K2.

Keeping 2 sts each side in St st for edges and continue in patterns as established, rep decrease row every 4th row 5{4-3-2} times more, then every 2nd row 9{13-17-21} times.

Bind off remaining sts. (Remember st counts vary depending on which pattern row you are on.)

FINISHING

Weave Front and Back to Sleeves along raglan lines *(Fig. 14, page 128)*.

Weave Sleeve and side seams.

Neckline trim: With circular needle and RS facing, beginning at right Back shoulder, pick up 70{76-82-88} sts along Back neck *(Figs. 13a & b, page 128)*, 32 sts along top of Left Sleeve, 70{76-82-88} sts along Front neck, then 32 sts along top of Right Sleeve — 204{216-228-240} sts; place marker and join.

Established Rib: (K2, P2) around.

Work rib for 2 rnds more.

Next (Cross) Rnd: * K2, P2, (RT, P2) 2 times; rep from * around.

Work in K2, P2 rib for 1 rnd.

Rep Cross Rnd.

Work in K2, P2 rib for 2 rnds.

Bind off in rib.

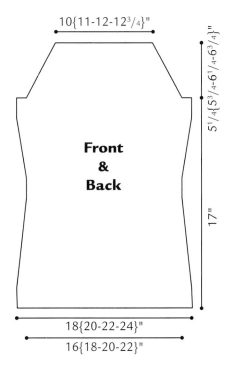

10{11-12-12³/₄}"

5¹/₄{5³/₄-6¹/₄-6³/₄}"

Front & Back

17"

18{20-22-24}"

16{18-20-22}"

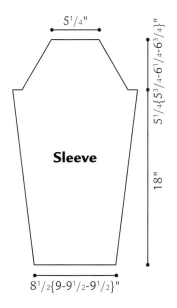

5¹/₄"

5¹/₄{5³/₄-6¹/₄-6³/₄}"

Sleeve

18"

8¹/₂{9-9¹/₂-9¹/₂}"

cozy CABLES

 **INTERMEDIATE**

SIZE
To fit Small{Medium-Large-Extra Large}.
Sample in size small.

FINISHED MEASUREMENTS
Bust at underarm:
38{42-46-50}"/96.5{106.5-117-127} cm
Length from back neck:
25{25$^1/_2$-26-26-$^1/_2$}"/63.5{65-66-67.5} cm

Size Note: Instructions are written for size Small with sizes Medium, Large, and Extra Large in braces { }. Instructions will be easier to read if you circle all the numbers pertaining to your size. If only one number is given, it applies to all sizes.

"This smooth textured cable lends subtle waves to this soft easy-to-knit, easy-to-wear boatneck sweater. Here I chose a luscious soft cotton that makes this version work well in summer, either in an air condtitioned office or at the breezy shoreline. In a soft wool, the sweater would be equally at home in snow, or in front of the fireplace."

MATERIALS

BLUE SKY ALPACAS **4** MEDIUM
"Dyed Cotton"
(100% Cotton; 100 grams/
150 yards)
Color #628 (Azul):
6{7-8-10} hanks
Straight knitting needles sizes,
8 (5 mm) **and** 9 (5.5 mm) **or**
size needed to obtain gauge
Cable needle (cn)
Stitch markers
Yarn needle

GAUGE

Over Stockinette st using larger
needles:
15 sts and 20 rows = 4" (10 cm)
Cable panel over 26 sts with
larger needles measures
approximately 5" (12.5 cm)
Take time to save time, check
your gauge.

PATTERN STITCHES

Back Knit Cross (BKC): Slip 1 st to cn and hold in back, K2
from LH needle, K1 from cn.
Front Knit Cross (FKC): Slip 2 sts to cn and hold in front, K1
from LH needle, K2 from cn.
Back Purl Cross (BPC): Slip 1 st to cn and hold in back, K2
from LH needle, P1 from cn.
Front Purl Cross (FPC): Slip 2 sts to cn and hold in front, P1
from LH needle, K2 from cn.

STOCKINETTE STITCH (St st): Any number of sts
Knit RS rows, purl WS rows.

K1, P1 RIB: Odd number of sts
Row 1 (RS): K2, P1, (K1, P1) across to last 2 sts, end K2.
Row 2: P2, K1, (P1, K1) across to last 2 sts, end P2.
Rep Rows 1 and 2 for K1, P1 Rib.

CABLE PATTERN: Multiple of 26 sts
Row 1 (WS): (K5, P 16, K5) across.
Row 2: (P4, BKC, K 12, FKC, P4) across.
Row 3 and all other WS rows: Knit all the knit sts, and
purl all the purl sts.
Row 4: (P3, BKC, K4, BPC, FPC, K4, FKC, P3) across.
Row 6: (P2, BKC, K4, BPC, P2, FPC, K4, FKC, P2) across.
Row 8: (P1, BKC, K4, BPC, P4, FPC, K4, FKC, P1) across.
Row 10: (BKC, K4, BPC, P6, FPC, K4, FKC) across.
Row 12: (K6, BPC, P8, FPC, K6) across
Row 14: (K6, FKC, P8, BKC, K6) across.
Row 16: (FPC, K4, FKC, P6, BKC, K4, BPC) across.
Row 18: (P1, FPC, K4, FKC, P4, BKC, K4, BPC, P1) across.
Row 20: (P2, FPC, K4, FKC, P2, BKC, K4, BPC, P2) across.
Row 22: (P3, FPC, K4, FKC, BKC, K4, BPC, P3) across.
Row 24: (P4, FPC, K 12, BPC, P4) across.
Rep Rows 1-24 for Cable Pattern.

Instructions begin on page 90.

BACK

With smaller needles, cast on 105{115-123-131} sts.

Work in K1, P1 Rib for 4 rows.

Knit RS row, decrease 9{11-11-11} sts evenly spaced *(see Decreases pages 126 & 127 and Decreasing Evenly Across A Row, page 126)* — 96{104-112-120} sts.

Change to larger needles.

Established Patterns (WS): Work 9{13-17-21} sts in St st, PM *(see Markers, page 124)*, work Row 1 of Cable Pattern over center 78 sts, PM, work 9{13-17-21} sts in St st.

Work even in patterns until piece measures 17^1/$_2$" (44.5 cm), end with a WS row.

Armhole Shaping: Bind off 4{4-4-5} sts at the beginning of the next 2 rows — 88{96-104-110} sts.

Next (decrease) Row (RS): K3, SSK *(Figs. 11a-c, page 127)*, work to last 5 sts, K2 tog *(Fig. 8, page 126)*, K3.

Work WS row as established.

Rep the last 2 rows 3{5-7-8} times more — 80{84-88-92} sts.

Work even until armhole measures 7^1/$_2${8-8^1/$_2$-9}"/ 19{20.5-21.5-23} cm, end with a WS row.

Back Neck and Shoulder Shaping: Mark center 52 sts.

Next Row (RS): Bind off 2{3-3-4} sts, work to center marked sts, join a second ball of yarn, bind off center 52 sts, work to end.

Working both sides at the same time with separate balls of yarn, bind off 2{3-3-4} sts at the beginning of the next 5{3-3-5} rows, then 0{2-4-0} sts at beginning of next 2 rows *(see Zeros, page 124)* AND AT THE SAME TIME, bind off 4 sts from each neck edge twice.

FRONT

Work same as for Back.

SLEEVES

With larger needles, cast on 34{36-38-40} sts.

Work in St st for 4 rows, end with a WS row.

Next (increase) Row (RS): K3, M1 *(Figs. 6a & b, page 126)*, knit across to last 3 sts, M1, K3.

Working increases into St st, rep increase row every 4th row 0{0-2-5} times, every 6th row 3{7-11-9} times, then every 8th row 7{4-0-0} times — 56{60-66-70} sts.

Work even until Sleeve measures 17^1/$_2$" (44.5 cm), end with a WS row.

Cap Shaping: Bind off 4{4-4-5} sts at the beginning of the next 2 rows — 48{52-58-60} sts.

Next (decrease) Row (RS): K3, SSK, work to last 5 sts, K2 tog, K3.

Purl WS row.

Rep the last 2 rows 12{13-15-16} more times.

Bind off 2{2-3-3} sts at the beginning of the next 4{2-4-4} rows, then 0{3-0-0} sts at beginning of next 2 rows.

Bind off remaining 14 sts.

FINISHING

Sew Front to Back at shoulder.

Weave side seams *(Fig. 14, page 128)*.

Back Neckline trim: With RS facing and smaller needles, pick up 60 sts evenly along Back neck edge *(Figs. 13a & b, page 128)*.

Purl 1 row, knit 1 row.

Bind off in purl.

Front Neckline trim: With RS facing and smaller needle, pick up 70 sts evenly along Front neck edge.

Purl 1 row, knit 1 row.

Bind off in purl.

Weave in ends and allow trim to roll to the RS.

Do not join trims where they meet.

Weave Sleeve seams.

Sew Sleeve caps into armholes.

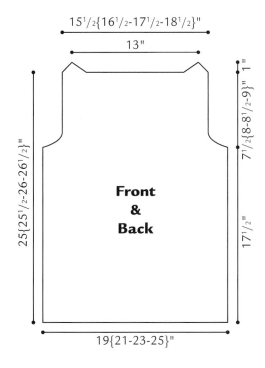

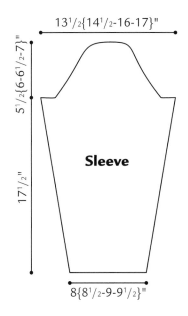

comforting CABLES

SIZES
To fit sizes Extra Small{Small-Medium-Large}.
Sample in size Small.

FINISHED MEASUREMENTS
Bust at underarm, slightly stretched:
33{37-39^1/$_2$-42}"/84{94-100.5-106.5} cm
Length from shoulder:
23{23^1/$_2$-24-24^1/$_2$}"/58.5{59.5-61-62} cm

Size Note: Instructions are written for size Extra Small with sizes Small, Medium, and Large in braces { }. Instructions will be easier to read if you circle all the numbers pertaining to your size. If only one number is given, it applies to all sizes.

❖

"For this design I wanted to achieve the silhouette of a '40's top: a sweetheart neckline, a cap sleeve, a slightly broad shouldered look. Instead of more complicated shaping, I used ribbing to shape the close fit.

"To modernize the look, I chose to mix uneven stripes of springtime colors in an organically dyed cotton. And even though this looks like lace at first glance, the central panel has an interesting and easy to work cable that lends some interesting surface texture."

MATERIALS

NASHUA HANDKNITS

"Natural Focus
Ecologie Cotton"

(100% Naturally Dyed Pima Cotton;
    50 grams/110 yards)
Color A: #NFE.0084 Acacia
    Yellow: 2{2-3-3} balls
Color B: #NFE.0080 Chestnut
    Brown: 2{3-3-3} balls
Color C: #NFE.0086 Logwood
    Grey: 2{2-2-2} balls
Color D: #NFE.0077 Robia
    Pink: 1{2-2-2} balls
Color E: #NFE.0082
    Sandalwood Brown:
        2{2-2-2} balls
Straight knitting needles,
    size 7 (4.5 mm) **or** size to
    obtain gauge
24" (61 cm) Circular knitting
    needle, size 7 (4.5 mm)
Stitch markers
Cable needle
Tapestry needle

GAUGE

K3, P2 Rib:
25 sts and 28 rows = 4" (10 cm)

Cabled Lace Panel:
22 sts and 28 rows = 4" (10 cm)

Take time to save time, check your
gauge.

PATTERN STITCHES

Cable 7 Front (C7F): Slip 3 sts to cn and hold in front, K4 from LH needle, K3 from cn.

K3, P2 RIB: Multiple of 5 sts plus 2
Row 1 (RS): P2, (K3, P2) across.
Row 2: K2, (P3, K2) across.
Rep Rows 1 and 2 for K3, P2 Rib.

SEED STITCH: Odd number of sts
All rows: K1, (P1, K1) across.

STOCKINETTE STITCH (St st): Any number of sts
Knit RS rows, purl WS rows.

CABLED LACE PATTERN:
Multiple of 10 sts plus 13
Row 1 (RS): K6, YO *(Fig. 3, page 125)*, SSK *(Figs. 11a-c, page 127)*, * K8, YO, SSK; rep from * across to last 5 sts, K5.
Row 2 and all other even numbered WS rows: Purl across.
Row 3: K4, K2 tog *(Fig. 8, page 126)*, YO, K1, YO, SSK, * K5, K2 tog, YO, K1, YO, SSK; rep from * across to last 4 sts, K4.
Row 5: K3, * K2 tog, YO, K3, YO, SSK, K3; rep from * across.
Row 7: K2, * K2 tog, YO, K5, YO, SSK, K1; rep from * across to last st, K1.
Row 9: K1, K2 tog, YO, K7, * YO, [slip 1, K2 tog, PSSO *(Figs. 12a & b, page 127)*], YO, K7; rep from * across to last 3 sts, YO, SSK, K1.
Row 11: K3, (C7F, K3) across.
Row 12: Purl across.
Rep Rows 1-12 for Cabled Lace Pattern.

COLOR SEQUENCE

* 10 rows B, 6 rows C, 10 rows D, 8 rows E, 10 rows A, 8 rows B, 6 rows C, 8 rows D, 6 rows E, 8 rows A; rep from *.

Note: Keep all edge sts, where noted, in St st.

Instructions begin on page 96.

BACK

Seed Border: With color B, cast on 99{111-119-127} sts.

Working in color sequence, knit 1 row, purl 1 row.

Eyelet Row (RS): K3, * YO, K2 tog, K2; rep from * across.

Purl WS row.

Change to Seed st and work until lower edge measures 3" (7.5 cm), end with a RS row.

Purl WS row, increase 12{10-12-14} sts evenly spaced *(see Increases and Increasing Evenly Across A Row, page 126)* — 111{121-131-141} sts.

Established Patterns (RS): K2 (edge sts), work Row 1 of K3, P2 Rib over 37{42-47-52} sts, PM *(see Markers, page 124)*, work Row 1 of Cabled Lace Pattern over center 33 sts, PM, work Row 1 of K3, P2 Rib over 37{42-47-52} sts, end K2 (edge sts).

Work even in patterns as established until piece measures 15$\frac{1}{2}$" (39.5 cm), end with a WS row.

Armhole Shaping: Bind off 6 sts at the beginning of the next 2 rows, then 2 sts at the beginning of the next 2 rows — 95{105-115-125} sts.

Next (decrease) Row (RS): K2, SSK, work to last 4 sts, K2 tog, K2.

Rep decrease row every RS 5{7-9-11} times more — 83{89-95-101} sts.

Work even until armhole measures 6$\frac{1}{2}${7-7$\frac{1}{2}$-8}"/ 16.5{18-19-20.5} cm, end with a WS row.

Back Neck Shaping: Mark center 21 sts.

Next Row (RS): Work as established to center 21 sts, join a second ball of yarn and bind off center 21 sts, work to end.

Working both sides at the same time with separate balls of yarn, bind off from each neck edge 4 sts 3 times AND AT THE SAME TIME, when armhole measures 7$\frac{1}{2}${8-8$\frac{1}{2}$-9}"/ 19{20.5-21.5-23} cm, end with a WS row.

Shoulder Shaping (RS): Bind off from each shoulder edge 6{7-8-9} sts twice, then 7{8-9-10} sts once.

FRONT

Work same as for Back until armhole measures approximately 1-2" (2.5-5 cm), ending with Row 12 of Cabled Lace Pattern.

Front Neck Shaping: Mark center 7 sts.

Continue armhole shaping as for Back and work in pattern to center 7 sts, K2 tog twice, join a second ball of yarn and K1, SSK, work to end (3 sts decreased).

Working both sides at once with separate balls of yarn, work WS row.

Next (decrease) Row (RS): Work to 3 sts before neck split, K2 tog, K1, on second side, K1, SSK, work to end.

Rep decrease row every RS row once more.

Work WS row.

Bind off 5 sts at each neck edge once, then 4 sts twice.

Work 2 rows even.

Next (decrease) Row (RS): Work to 3 sts before neck split, K2 tog, K1, on second side, K1, SSK, work to end.

Rep decrease row every 4th row 5 times more — 19{22-25-28} sts each side.

Work even until piece measures same as Back to shoulders.

Work shoulder shaping as for Back.

SLEEVES

Seed Border: With color B, cast on 67{71-79-87} sts.

Working in color sequence, knit 1 row, purl 1 row.

Eyelet Row (RS): K3, * YO, K2 tog, K2; rep from * across.

Purl WS row.

Change to Seed st and work until lower edge measures 1¹/₂" (4 cm) from eyelet row, end with a RS row.

Purl WS row, increase 9{10-12-9} sts evenly spaced — 76{81-91-96} sts.

Next Row (RS): K2 (edge sts), work K3, P2 Rib over center 72{77-87-92} sts, end K2 (edge sts).

Work even until piece measures 2¹/₂" (6.5 cm), end with a WS row.

Cap Shaping: Bind off 6 sts at the beginning of the next 2 rows, then 2 sts at the beginning of the next 2 rows — 60{65-75-80} sts.

Next (decrease) Row (RS): K1, SSK, work to last 3 sts, K2 tog, K1.

Keeping 2 edge sts each side, rep decrease row every 2nd row 4{4-18-20} times more, every 4th row 3{3-0-0} times *(see Zeros, page 124)*, then every 2nd row 4{6-0-0} times — 36{37-37-38} sts.

Bind off 2 sts at beginning of next 2 rows, then 3 sts at beginning of next 2 rows.

Bind off remaining 26{27-27-28} sts.

FINISHING

Sew Front to Back at shoulders.

Weave side seams and Sleeve seams *(Fig. 14, page 128)*.

Sew Sleeve caps into armhole, easing in any fullness.

Neckline trim: With circular needle, RS facing and A, beginning at bound-off section on Right Front, pick up 41 sts to shoulder, 44 sts along Back neck, and 41 sts to the end of bound-off section on Left Front. Purl 1 row. Knit 1 row AND AT THE SAME TIME, work K2 tog at each corner of Front neck.

Bind off in knit.

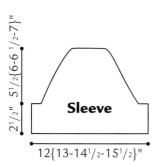

Sleeve

2¹/₂" 5¹/₂{6-6¹/₂-7}"

12{13-14¹/₂-15¹/₂}"

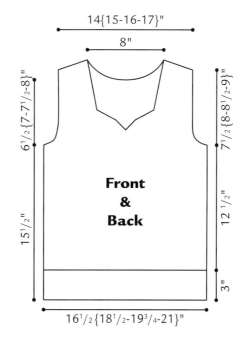

Front & Back

14{15-16-17}"

8"

6¹/₂{7-7¹/₂-8}"

7¹/₂{8-8¹/₂-9}"

15¹/₂"

12 ¹/₂"

3"

16¹/₂{18¹/₂-19³/₄-21}"

cabled
CONTOURS

SIZES
To fit sizes Small{Medium-Large-Extra Large}.
Sample in size Small.

FINISHED MEASUREMENTS
Bust at underarm:
38{42-46-50}"/96.5{106.5-117-127} cm
Length from back neck:
27{27^1/$_2$-28-28^1/$_2$}"/68.5{70-71-72.5} cm

Size Note: Instructions are written for size Small with sizes Medium, Large, and Extra Large in braces { }. Instructions will be easier to read if you circle all the numbers pertaining to your size. If only one number is given, it applies to all sizes.

"I love the challenge of making the classic cabled sweater look fresh! How about shortening the sleeves? And adding a big, deeply ribbed and shaped collar? And a belt and buckle to make it more tailored?

"Here I designed my own cable that is not in the traditional pattern books: it has depth and texture, but incorporates some twists in a combination that has never seen print before!

"Any springy wool would work for this sweater, but the thick-and-thin quality of this one, with the soft shading of the organic dye, makes the texture unique."

MATERIALS
NASHUA HANDKINTS  (MEDIUM 4)
"Ecologie Wool"
(100% Naturally Dyed Wool;
50 grams/87 yards
  Color #NFW80 (Chestnut):
  17{19-21-23} balls
Straight knitting needles, size
  9 (5.5 mm) **or** size needed to
  obtain gauge
36" (91.5 cm) Circular knitting
  needle, size 9 (5.5 mm)
Cable needle (cn)
Stitch markers
Yarn needle
Sewing needle and
  matching thread
$1^1/_8$" (3 cm) Buttons - 4
$1^1/_2$-2" (4-5 cm) Buckle

GAUGE
Over Textured Pattern:
18 sts and 28 rows = 4" (10 cm)
Cable Panel over 24 sts
measures approximately $3^1/_2$"
(9 cm) wide.
Take time to save time, check
your gauge.

PATTERN STITCHES
Front Cross 8 (FC8): Slip 4 sts to cn and hold in front, K4 from LH needle, K4 from cn.
Back Cross 8 (BC8): Slip 4 sts to cn and hold in back, K4 from LH needle, K4 from cn.
Twist 6 Back (T6B): Slip 2 sts to cn and hold in back, K4 from LH needle, P2 from cn.
Twist 6 Front (T6F): Slip 4 sts to cn and hold in front, P2 from LH needle, K4 from cn.

K2, P2 RIB: Multiple of 4 sts plus 2
Row 1 (RS): K2, (P2, K2) across.
Row 2: P2, (K2, P2) across.
Rep Rows 1 and 2 for K2, P2 Rib.

STOCKINETTE STITCH (St st): Any number of sts
Knit RS rows, purl WS rows.

TEXTURED PATTERN: Odd number of sts
Row 1 (RS): Knit across.
Row 2: Purl across.
Row 3: K1, (P1, K1) across.
Row 4: P1, (K1, P1) across.
Row 5: Knit across.
Row 6: Purl across.
Row 7: P1, (K1, P1) across.
Row 8: K1, (P1, K1) across.
Rep Rows 1-8 for Textured Pattern.

CABLE PANEL: Over 24 sts

Rows 1, 3, 5, 7 (RS): P4, K4, P3, K2, P3, K4, P4.

Rows 2, 4, 6, 8: Knit the knit sts and purl the purl sts.

Row 9: P4, FC8, BC8, P4.

Row 10: K4, P 16, K4.

Rows 11-20: Rep Rows 1-10.

Row 21: P2, T6B, FC8, T6F, P2.

Row 22: K2, P4, K2, P8, K2, P4, K2.

Row 23: P2, K4, P2, K8, P2, K4, P2.

Row 24: K2, P4, K2, P8, K2, P4, K2.

Row 25: T6B, P2, K8, P2, T6F.

Row 26: P4, K4, P8, K4, P4.

Row 27: K4, P4, FC8, P4, K4.

Row 28: P4, K4, P8, K4, P4.

Row 29: K4, P4, K8, P4, K4.

Row 30: P4, K4, P8, K4, P4.

Row 31: FC8, K8, BC8.

Row 32: K4, P16, K4.

Row 33: P4, K4, FC8, K4, P4.

Row 34: K4, P 16, K4,

Rep Rows 1-34 for Cable Panel.

Note: Keep all edge sts, where noted, in St st.

Instructions begin on page 102.

BACK

Cast on 118{126-138-146} sts.

Work even in K2, P2 Rib for 4" (10 cm), decrease 11 sts evenly on last WS row **(see Decreases, pages 126 & 127 and Decreasing Evenly Across A Row, page 126)** — 107{115-127-135} sts.

Established Patterns (RS): K2 (edge sts), PM **(see Markers, page 124)**, beginning all patterns with Row 1, work Textured Pattern over 25{29-35-39} sts, PM, work Cable Panel over 24 sts, PM, work Textured Pattern over center 5 sts, PM, work Cable Panel over 24 sts, PM, work Textured Pattern over 25{29-35-39} sts, PM, end K2 (edge sts).

Work even until 20 rows have been completed above rib, end with a WS row.

Side Shaping (decrease) Row (RS): K1, SSK **(Figs. 11a-c, page 127)**, work to last 3 sts, K2 tog **(Fig. 8, page 126)**, K1.

Keeping 2 sts each end in St st, rep decrease row every 14th row 3 times more — 99{107-119-127} sts.

Work even until piece measures 14½" (37 cm), end with a WS row.

Side Shaping (increase) Row (RS): K2, M1 **(Figs. 6a & b, page 126)**, work to last 2 sts, M1, K2.

Keeping 2 sts each end in St st, rep increase row every 8th row 3 times more — 107{115-127-135} sts.

Work even until piece measures 21" (53.5 cm), end with a WS row.

Raglan Shaping: Bind off 4 sts at the beginning of the next 2 rows — 99{107-119-127} sts.

Work 2 rows even.

Next (decrease) Row (RS): K2, SSK, work to last 4 sts, K2 tog, K2.

Keeping 2 sts each end in St st, work even for 3 more rows.

Bind off 2 sts at the beginning of the next 34{38-40-46} rows, then 0{0-3-0} sts at beginning of next 2 rows **(see Zeros, page 124)**.

Bind off remaining 29{29-31-33} sts on last RS row.

LEFT FRONT

Cast on 58{62-70-74} sts.

Work even in K2, P2 Rib for 4" (10 cm), decrease 5{5-7-7} sts evenly on last WS row — 53{57-63-67} sts.

Next Row (RS): K2 (edge sts), PM, beginning all patterns with Row 1, work Textured Pattern over 25{29-35-39} sts, PM, work Cable over 24 sts, PM, end K2 (edge sts).

Work even until 20 rows have been completed above rib, end with a WS row.

Side Shaping (decrease) Row (RS): K1, SSK, work to end.

Keeping first and last 2 sts in St st rep decrease row every 14th row 3 times more — 49{53-59-63} sts.

Work even until piece measures 14½" (37 cm), end with a WS row.

Side Shaping (increase) Row (RS): K2, M1, work to end.

Keeping first and last 2 sts in St st, work even for 7 rows more.

Instructions continued on page 104.

Side and V-Neck Shaping (RS): K2, M1, work to last 3 sts, K2 tog, K1.

Continue to increase at beginning of RS rows every 8th row 2 times more AND AT THE SAME TIME, decrease at V-neck edge (end of RS rows) as described every 4th row 14 times more, then every RS row 3{3-5-5} times.

Work even until piece measures 21" (53.5 cm), end with a WS row.

Raglan shaping (RS): Bind off 4 sts at the beginning of RS row.

Continue decreases at V neck AND AT THE SAME TIME, work 3 rows even.

Next (decrease) Row (RS): K2, SSK, work to end.

Keeping first and last 2 sts in St st, work even for 3 more rows.

Bind off 2 sts at the beginning of the next 14{16-18-20} RS rows.

Bind off remaining 2 sts on last RS row.

RIGHT FRONT
Work same as for Left Front, reversing all patterns and shaping.

RIGHT SLEEVE
Cast on 78{82-86-94} sts.

Work even in K2, P2 Rib for 2¹/₂" (6.5 cm), decrease 8 sts evenly on last WS row — 70{74-78-86} sts.

Established Patterns (RS): K2 (edge sts), PM, beginning all patterns with Row 1, work Textured Pattern over 21{23-25-29} sts, PM, work Cable Panel over center 24 sts, PM, work Textured Pattern over 21{23-25-29} sts, PM, end K2 (edge sts).

Work in patterns as established until Sleeve measures 8" (20.5 cm), end with a WS row.

Raglan Cap Shaping: Bind off 4 sts at the beginning of the next 2 rows — 62{66-70-78} sts.

Work 2 rows even.

Next (decrease) Row (RS): K2, SSK, work to last 4 sts, K2 tog, K2.

Keeping first and last 3 sts in St st, work even for 3 more rows.

Rep last 4 rows 0{0-1-0} times more.

Rep decrease row every RS row 14{16-16-20} times more — 32{32-34-36} sts.

Work WS row.

Top of Cap Shaping (RS): Bind off 7{7-7-8} sts at the beginning of the next 3{3-1-3} RS rows, then 8{8-8-9} sts on next 1{1-3-1} RS rows AND AT THE SAME TIME, continue to decrease at the end of the next 3 RS rows.

LEFT SLEEVE
Work same as for Right Sleeve, reversing top of cap shaping.

FINISHING
Weave Fronts and Back to Sleeves along raglan lines (*Fig. 14, page 128*).

Weave side and Sleeve seams.

Left Front band: With RS facing, beginning at V-Neck shaping, pick up 70{72-74-76} sts along left Front edge (*Fig. 13a, page 128*).

Knit 2 rows, purl 3 rows, knit 3 rows, purl 1 row.

Bind off in knit.

Right Front band: Work same as for left band, but make four 3-st buttonholes on first RS row as follows (by binding off 3 sts and casting on 3 sts on next row): K8{10-12-14}, make 3-st buttonhole, * K 16, make 3-st buttonhole; rep from * across to last 2 sts, K2.

Collar: With circular needle and RS facing, pick up 195{195-201-207} sts evenly around neck edge *(Fig. 13b, page 128)*.

Established Rib (RS of collar): K3, (P3, K3) across.

Next Row: P3, (K3, P3) across.

Short Rows: Work 111{111-117-123} sts, yarn forward (yf), slip 1, yarn back (yb), turn, slip st back to RH needle, work 27 sts, * yf, slip 1, yb, turn, slip st to RH needle, work to wrapped st, lift the yarn that wraps the st, and work wrapped st tog with yarn that surrounds it, work 2 more sts; rep from * continuing to work 2 more sts beyond wrapped st every row until all sts have been worked.

Rib as established over all sts for 3 more rows.

Bind off.

Belt: Cast on 9 sts.

Next Row (RS): K2, P1, (K1, P1) 2 times, K2.

Next Row (WS): Knit the knit sts and purl the purl sts as they appear.

Rep these 2 rows until belt measures 36" (91.5 cm), end with a WS row.

Next Row (RS): K1, SSK, K1, P1, K1, K2 tog, K1.

Next Row (WS): P3, K1, P3.

Next Row (RS): K1, SSK, P1, K2 tog, K1.

Next Row (WS): P2, K1, P2.

Next Row (RS): K1, [slip 1, K2 tog, PSSO *(Figs. 12a & b, page 127)*], K1.

Cut yarn and thread through remaining 3 sts.

Weave end to back.

Steam belt and sew cast on edge through belt buckle.

Side belt loops (make 2): Cast on 13 sts.

Bind off.

Sew to each side.

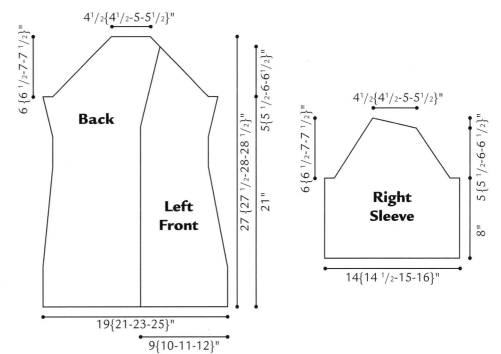

4¹/₂{4¹/₂-5-5¹/₂}"

6{6¹/₂-7-7¹/₂}"

5{5¹/₂-6-6¹/₂}"

Back

Left Front

27{27¹/₂-28-28¹/₂}"

21"

19{21-23-25}"

9{10-11-12}"

4¹/₂{4¹/₂-5-5¹/₂}"

6{6¹/₂-7-7¹/₂}"

5{5¹/₂-6-6¹/₂}"

Right Sleeve

8"

14{14¹/₂-15-16}"

family CABLES

●■■■▢ INTERMEDIATE

PATTERN STITCHES
(For All Sweaters)

Back Cross (BC): Slip 6 sts to cn and hold in back, K6 from LH needle, K6 from cn.

Front Cross (FC): Slip 6 sts to cn and hold in front, K6 from LH needle, K6 from cn.

STOCKINETTE STITCH (St st):
Any number of sts
Knit RS rows, purl WS rows.

K2, P2 RIB: Multiple of 4 sts plus 2
Row 1 (RS): K2, (P2, K2) across.
Row 2: P2, (K2, P2) across.
Rep Rows 1 and 2 for K2, P2 Rib.

SHADOW RIB: Multiple of 4 sts plus 3
Row 1 (RS): P3, * K tbl (*Fig. 4, page 125*), P3; rep from * across.
Row 2: Knit across.
Rep Rows 1 and 2 for Shadow Rib.

THICK RIB: Multiple of 4 sts plus 3
Row 1 (RS): P3, * K1 in the row below, P3; rep from * across.
Row 2: Knit across.
Rep Rows 1 and 2 for Thick Rib.

LARGE STRIPED PATTERN:
Any number of sts
Row 1 (RS): With A, knit across.
Row 2: Knit across.

Woman's Cardigan
Shown on page 117.

Rows 3, 5, 7, 9, 11, 13 (RS): Purl across.
Rows 4, 6, 8, 10, 12 and 14 (WS): Knit across.
Rows 15-28: Change to B, rep Rows 1-14.
Rep Rows 1- 28 for Large Striped Pattern.

SMALL STRIPED PATTERN:
Any number of sts
Rows 1 and 3 (RS): With A, purl across.
Rows 2 and 4: Knit across.
Rows 5 and 7 (RS): Change to B, purl across.
Rows 6 and 8: Knit across.
Rep Rows 1-8 for Small Striped Pattern.

BACK CROSS CABLE: Over 12 sts
Row 1 (RS): With A, K 12.
Row 2 and all WS rows: P 12.
Rows 3 and 5: K 12.
Row 7: BC.
Row 9, 11 and 13: K 12.
Row 14: P 12.
Rows 15-28: Change B, rep Rows 1-14.
Rep Rows 1-28 for Back Cross Cable.

FRONT CROSS CABLE: Over 12 sts
Work same as for Back Cross Cable, except on Row 7 work FC instead of BC.

Note: Keep all edge sts, where noted, in St st.

man's PULLOVER

To fit sizes Small{Medium-Large-ExtraLarge}.
Sample in size Medium.

FINISHED MEASUREMENTS
Chest at underarm:
 40{44-48-52}"/101.5{112-122-132} cm
Length from back neck:
25$\frac{1}{2}${26-26$\frac{1}{2}$-27}"/65{66-67.5-68.5} cm

Size Note: Instructions are written for size Small with sizes Medium, Large, and Extra Large in braces { }. Instructions will be easier to read if you circle all the numbers pertaining to your size. If only one number is given, it applies to all sizes.

"When designing this sporty group of sweaters, I found it an interesting challenge to make each sweater a little bit different. To lend variety, I used the same patterns in several ways, and applied several colors in two different striped patterns! Each sweater shares the same easy cable, but placed in a different way."

"The man's sweater uses all the same patterns in a totally different way, divided by a yoke."

109

MATERIALS

BERROCO MEDIUM 4
"Comfort"
(50% Superfine Nylon, 50%
Superfine Acrylic;
100 grams/104 yards)
   A: #9762 (Spruce):
      2{3-3-3} skeins
   B: #9744 (Teal):
      4{4-5-5} skeins
Straight knitting needles, sizes
   7 (4.5 mm) **and** 8 (5 mm) **or**
   size needed to obtain gauge
16" (40.5 cm) Circular knitting
   needle, size 7 (4.5 mm)
Cable needle (cn)
Stitch markers
Yarn needle

GAUGE

Over St st with larger needles:
17 sts and 24 rows = 4" (10 cm)
Over Shadow Rib with larger
needles:
18 sts and 24 rows = 4" (10 cm)
Take time to save time, check
your gauge.

Note: Refer to Pattern Stitches,
page 106.

BACK

With smaller needles and A, cast
on 106{114-122-130} sts.

Work in K2, P2 Rib until piece
measures 2^1/$_2$" (6.5 cm),
decrease 7 sts on last RS row —
99{107-115-123} sts.

Change to larger needles and B.

Purl WS row.

Note: In this section, work Back
and Front Cross Cables in Color
B only. Begin and end Shadow
Rib with P2 instead of P3.

Established Patterns (RS): K2
(edge sts), beginning with Row 1
for all patterns, work Shadow Rib
over 29{33-37-41} sts, PM *(see
Markers, page 124)*, Back Cross
Cable over 12 sts, PM, Shadow
Rib over center 13 sts,
PM, Front Cross Cable over
12 sts, PM, Shadow Rib over
29{33-37-41} sts, end K2 (edge
sts).

Keeping in patterns as
established, work even until
28 rows of Cable Patterns have
been completed 2 times and
Rows 1-14 once (70 rows) [piece
measures approximately 13"
(33 cm)], end with a WS row.

Change to A.

Note: In this section, work Back
and Front Cross Cables in Colors
as noted in pattern.

Change Patterns (RS): K2
(edge sts), beginning with
Row 1 for all patterns, work
Large Striped Pattern over
29{33-37-41} sts AND AT THE
SAME TIME decrease 1 st in
this section [28{32-36-40} sts
remaining], slip marker, Back
Cross Cable over 12 sts, slip
marker, Large Striped Pattern
over center 13 sts, slip marker,
Front Cross Cable over 12 sts,
slip marker, Large Striped Pattern
over 29{33-37-41} sts AND AT
THE SAME TIME decrease 1 st
in this section [{28-32-36-40} sts
remaining], end K2 (edge sts) —
97{105-113-121} sts.

Keeping in patterns as
established, work even until piece
measures 25^1/$_2${26-26^1/$_2$-27}"/
65{66-67.5-68.5} cm, end with a
WS row.

**Back Neck and Shoulder
Shaping (RS):** Mark center
13{13-15-17} sts.

Next Row (RS): Bind off
9{10-11-12} sts, work to marked
sts and join a second ball of yarn,
bind off center 13{13-15-17} sts,
work to end.

Working both sides at the same
time with separate balls of
yarn, bind off 9{10-11-12} sts
at the beginning of the next
3{5-5-5} rows, then 8{0-0-0} sts
at beginning of next 2 rows *(see
Zeros, page 124)* AND AT THE
SAME TIME, bind off 8 sts from
each neck edge twice.

FRONT

Work same as for Back until piece measures 23$\frac{1}{2}${24-24$\frac{1}{2}$-25}"/ 59.5{61-62-63.5} cm, end with a WS row.

Front Neck Shaping (RS):
Mark center 13{13-15-17} sts.

Next Row (RS): Work to marked sts and join a second ball of yarn, bind off center 13{13-15-17} sts, work to end.

Working both sides at the same time with separate balls of yarn, bind off at each neck edge 4 sts 3 times, then 2 sts 2 times AND AT THE SAME TIME, when Front measures same as Back to shoulder, end with a WS row.

Shoulder Shaping (RS):
Bind off 9{10-11-12} sts at the beginning of the next 4{6-6-6} rows, then 8{0-0-0} sts at beginning of next 2 rows.

SLEEVES

With smaller needles and A, cast on 46{46-50-50} sts.

Work in K2, P2 Rib until piece measures 2" (5 cm), decrease 3 sts on last RS row *(see Decreases, pages 126 & 127 and Decreasing Evenly Across A Row, page 126)* — 43{43-47-47} sts.

Change to larger needles and B.

Purl WS row.

Established Patterns
(RS): K2 (edge sts), work Row 1 of Shadow Rib over 39{39-43-43} sts, end K2 (edge sts).

Work even for 3 more rows.

Next (increase) Row (RS): K2, M1 *(Figs. 6a & b, page 126)*, work to last 2 sts, M1, K2: 45{45-49-49} cm.

Working increases into Shadow Rib, rep increase row every 4th row 0{0-0-6} times, every 6th row 11{19-19-15} times, then every 8th row 6{0-0-0} times AND AT THE SAME TIME, continue even until piece measures approximately 21" (53.5 cm), decrease 4 sts on last WS row.

Change to A.

Next Row (RS): K2 (edge sts), work in Small Striped Pattern to last 2 sts, K2 (edge sts).

Continue as established, working any remaining side increases into Small Striped Pattern, until Sleeve measures 23" (58.5 cm) — 75{79-83-87} sts.

Bind off.

FINISHING

Sew Front to Back at shoulders.

Neckline rib: With circular needle and B, beginning at right shoulder seam, pick up 108{108-112-116} sts evenly around neckline edge *(Figs. 13a & b, page 128)*; place marker and join.

Work in rnds of K2, P2 Rib for 3 rnds, change to A for 4 rnds, change to B for 2 rnds.

Bind off.

Tie markers 8$\frac{1}{2}${9-9$\frac{1}{2}$-10}"/ 21.5{23-24-25.5} cm down from shoulders on Front and Back.

Sew Sleeve tops between markers.

Weave Sleeve and side seams *(Fig. 14, page 128)*.

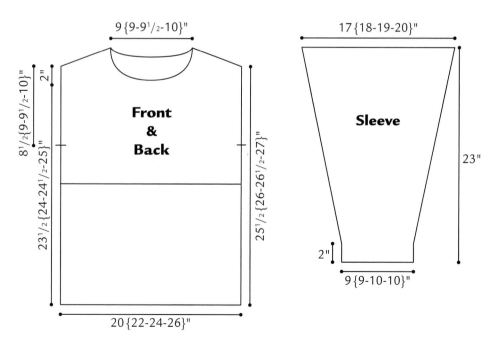

child's
PULLOVER

To fit sizes Small (2-4){Medium (6-8)-Large (10-12)}.
Sample in size Medium.

FINISHED MEASUREMENTS
Chest at underarm:
28{32-36}"/71{81.5-91.5} cm
Length from back neck:
15{16-18}"/38{40.5-45.5} cm

Size Note: Instructions are written for size Small with sizes Medium
and Large in braces { }. Instructions will be easier to read if you
circle all the numbers pertaining to your size. If only one number is
given, it applies to all sizes.

"For the child's pullover I used several colors—in fact this design would be a great way to
use up small amounts of yarn of the same weight and gauge."

MATERIALS

BERROCO "Comfort"

MEDIUM 4

(50% Superfine Nylon,
50% Superfine Acrylic;
100 grams/104 yards)
  A: #9757 (Lillet):
    2{2-2} skeins
  B: #9721 (Sprig):
    2{2-2} skeins
  C: #9724 (Pumpkin):
    2{2-2}skeins
Straight knitting needles, sizes
  7 (4.5 mm) **and** 8 (5 mm) **or**
  size needed to obtain gauge
16" (40.5 cm) Circular knitting
  needle, size 7 (4.5 mm)
Cable needle (cn)
Stitch markers
Yarn needle

GAUGE

Over St st with larger needles:
17 sts and 24 rows = 4" (10 cm)
Over Thick Rib with larger
needles:
18 sts and 24 rows = 4" (10 cm)
Take time to save time, check
your gauge.

Note: Refer to Pattern Stitches,
page 106.

BACK

With smaller needles and C, cast
on 74{82-90} sts.

Work K2, P2 Rib until piece
measures 2" (5 cm), decrease
2 sts on last WS row *(see
Decreases, pages 126 & 127 and
Decreasing Evenly Across A Row,
page 126)* — 72{80-88} sts.

Change to larger needles and A.

Established Patterns (RS):
K2 (edge sts), beginning with
Row 1 for all patterns, work
Large Striped Pattern over
18{22-26} sts, PM *(see Markers,
page 124)*, Back Cross Cable
over 12 sts, PM, Large Striped
Pattern over center 8 sts, PM,
Front Cross Cable over 12 sts,
PM, Large Striped Pattern over
18{22-26} sts, end K2 (edge sts).

Keeping in patterns as
established, work even until piece
measures 15{16-18}"/
38{40.5-45.5} cm, end with a WS
row.

**Back Neck and Shoulders
Shaping:** Mark center
20{20-22} sts.

Next Row (RS): Bind off
5{7-8} sts, work to marked sts
and join a second ball of yarn,
bind off center 20{20-22} sts,
work to end.

Working both sides at the same
time with separate balls of
yarn, bind off 5{7-8} sts at the
beginning of the next 3 rows,
then 6{6-7} sts at the beginning
of the last 2 rows AND AT THE
SAME TIME, bind off 5 sts from
each neck edge twice.

FRONT

With smaller needles and A, cast
on 74{82-90} sts.

Work K2, P2 Rib until piece
measures 2" (5 cm), decrease
2 sts on last WS row —
72{80-88} sts.

Change to larger needles and C.

Note: Replace A with C in Large
Striped Pattern and Back and
Front Cross Cables for Front.

Established Patterns (RS):
K2 (edge sts), beginning with
Row 1 for all patterns, work
Large Striped Pattern over
18{22-26} sts, PM, Back Cross
Cable over 12 sts, PM, Large
Striped Pattern over center 8 sts,
PM, Front Cross Cable over
12 sts, PM, Large Striped Pattern
over 18{22-26} sts, end K2 (edge
sts).

Keeping in patterns as established,
work even until piece measures
12$\frac{1}{2}${13$\frac{1}{2}$-15$\frac{1}{2}$}"/
32{34.5-39.5} cm, end with
a WS row.

Front Neck Shaping: Mark
center 16{16-18} sts.

Next Row (RS): Work to
marked sts and join a second
ball of yarn, bind off center
16{16-18} sts, work to end.

Working both sides at the same time with separate balls of yarn, bind off 3 sts at each neck edge 4 times AND AT THE SAME TIME, when Front measures same as Back to shoulder, end with a WS row.

Shoulder Shaping (RS): Bind off 5{7-8} sts at the beginning of the next 4 rows, then 6{6-7} sts at the beginning of the last 2 rows.

LEFT SLEEVE
With larger needles and C, cast on 31{31-35} sts.

Knit 1 row, purl 1 row.

Next Row (RS): K2 (edge sts), work in Thick Rib over center 27{27-31} sts, K2 (edge sts).

Work even as established for 3 more rows.

Next (increase) Row (RS): K2, M1 *(Figs. 6a & b, page 126)*, work to last 2 sts, M1, K2.

Working increases into pattern, rep increase row every 6th row 10{12-12} times more AND AT THE SAME TIME, when piece measures 3" (7.5 cm), end with a WS row.

Change to A.

Next Row (RS): Change to Small Striped Pattern, working any remaining side increases into Small Striped Pattern until Sleeve measures 12{13-14}"/30.5{33-35.5} cm, end with a WS row.

Bind off 53{57-61} sts.

RIGHT SLEEVE
With larger needles and A, cast on 31{31-35} sts.

Work as for Left Sleeve except replace A with B and B with C in Small Striped Pattern for Right Sleeve.

FINISHING
Sew Front to Back at shoulders.

Neckline edge: With RS facing, circular needle and A, beginning at right shoulder seam, pick up 96{96-100} sts evenly around neckline edge *(Figs. 13a & b, page 128)*; place marker and join.

Work in rnds of K2, P2 Rib for 3 rnds, change to C for 4 rnds, then change to B for 2 rnds.

Bind off.

Tie markers 6{6½-7}"/15{16.5-18} cm down from shoulders on Front and Back.

Sew Sleeve tops between markers.

Weave Sleeve and side seams *(Fig. 14, page 128)*.

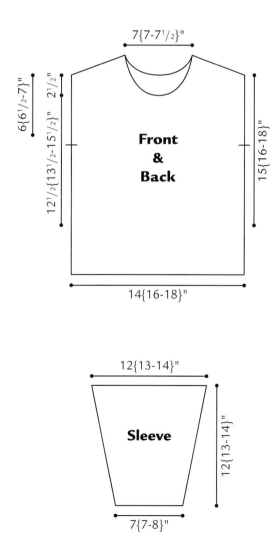

7{7-7½}"

6{6½-7}"

2½"

12½{13½-15½}"

15{16-18}"

Front & Back

14{16-18}"

12{13-14}"

Sleeve

12{13-14}"

7{7-8}"

115

woman's
CARDIGAN

To fit sizes Small{Medium-Large-Extra Large}.
Sample in size Small.

FINSIHED MEASUREMENTS

Bust at underarm, buttoned: 36{40-44-48}"/91.5{101.5-112-122} cm
Length from back neck: 18^1/$_2${19-19^1/$_2$-20}"/47{48.5-49.5-51} cm

Size Note: Instructions are written for size Small with sizes Medium, Large, and Extra Large in braces { }. Instructions will be easier to read if you circle all the numbers pertaining to your size. If only one number is given, it applies to all sizes.

"The woman's sweater—not necessarily for Mom—varies color placement from back to front, sharing colors with the child's sweater."

MATERIALS
BERROCO "Comfort"
(50% Superfine Nylon,
50% Superfine Acrylic;
100 grams/104 yards)
A: #9757 (Lillet):
   2{2-3-3} skeins
B: #9730 (Teaberry):
   4{4-5-5} skeins
Straight knitting needles sizes,
   7 (4.5 mm) **and** 8 (5 mm) **or**
   size needed to obtain gauge
Cable needle (cn)
Stitch markers
Yarn needle
Sewing needle and matching
   thread
1¼" (3 cm) Buttons - 4

GAUGE
Over St st with larger needles:
17 sts and 24 rows = 4" (10 cm)
Over Thick Rib with larger
needles: 18 sts and 24 rows = 4"
(10 cm)
Take time to save time, check
your gauge.

Note: Refer to Pattern Stitches, page 106.

BACK
With smaller needles and B, cast on 94{102-110-118} sts.

Work in K2, P2 Rib until piece measures 2" (5 cm), decrease 5 sts on last WS row **(see Decreases, pages 126 & 127 and Decreasing Evenly Across A Row, page 126)** — 89{97-105-113} sts.

Change to larger needles and A.

Established Patterns (RS): K2 (edge sts), beginning with Row 1 for all patterns, work Large Striped Pattern over 24{28-32-36} sts, PM **(see Markers, page 124)**, Back Cross Cable over 12 sts, PM, Large Striped Pattern over center 13 sts, PM, Front Cross Cable over 12 sts, PM, Large Striped Pattern over 24{28-32-36} sts, end K2 (edge sts).

Keeping in patterns as established, work even until piece measures 11" (28 cm), end with a WS row.

Armhole Shaping: Bind off 4{4-5-5} sts at the beginning of the next 2 rows — 81{89-95-103} sts.

Decrease 1 st each end of the next 3{5-6-8} RS rows — 75{79-83-87} sts.

Work even until armhole measures 7½{8-8½-9}"/ 19{20.5-21.5-23} cm, ending with a RS row.

Back Neck and Shoulder Shaping: Mark center 11 sts.

Next Row (RS): Bind off 5{6-7-7} sts, work to marked st and join a second ball of yarn, bind off center 11 sts, work to end.

Working both sides at the same time with separate balls of yarn bind off 5{6-7-7} sts at the beginning of the next 3 rows, then 6{6-6-8} sts at the beginning of the next 2 rows AND AT THE SAME TIME, bind off 8 sts from each neck edge twice.

Instructions continued on page 120.

LEFT FRONT

With smaller needles and A, cast on 46{50-54-58} sts.

Work in K2, P2 Rib until piece measures 2" (5 cm), decrease 3 sts on last WS row — 43{47-51-55} sts.

Change to larger needles and B.

Note: Replace A with B and B with A in Large Striped Pattern and Cable Patterns for Fronts.

Established Patterns (RS): K2 (edge sts), beginning with Row 1 for all patterns, work Large Striped Pattern over 24{28-32-36} sts, PM, Back Cross Cable over 12 sts, PM, Large Striped Pattern over 3 sts, end K2 (edge sts).

Keeping in patterns as established, work even until piece measures 11" (28 cm), end with a WS row.

Armhole Shaping (RS): Bind off 4{4-5-5} sts at the beginning of the next RS row.

Decrease 1 st beginning of the next 3{5-6-8} RS rows — 36{38-40-42} sts.

Work even until armhole measures 5{5½-6-6½}"/12.5{14-15-16.5} cm, end with a RS row.

Front Neck Shaping (WS): Bind off at Front neck edge 10 sts once, 3 sts twice, then 2 sts twice — 16{18-20-22} sts.

Work even until armhole measures same as Back to shoulder, end with a WS row.

Shoulder shaping (RS): Bind off at shoulder edge 5{6-7-7} sts 2 times, then 6{6-6-8} sts once.

RIGHT FRONT

Work same as for Left Front, same color sequence, reversing pattern PLACEMENTS and shaping and use Front Cross Cable instead of Back Cross Cable.

SLEEVES

With larger needles and A, cast on 39{39-43-43} sts.

Knit 1 row, purl 1 row.

Change to B.

Note: Replace A with B and B with A in Small Striped Pattern for Sleeves.

Next Row: Work in Small Striped Pattern until 6 stripes are complete, end with an A stripe.

Piece should measure approximately 4" (10 cm).

Change to B and knit RS row, increase 4 sts evenly — 43{43-47-47} sts
.

Established Pattern (WS): P2 (edge sts), beginning with Row 2, work Thick Rib Pattern over 39{39-43-43} sts, end P2 (edge sts).

Continue as established for 4 more rows.

Next (increase) Row (RS):
K2, M1 *(Figs. 6a & b, page 126)*, work to last 2 sts, M1, K2.

Working increases into pattern, rep increase row every 4th row 0{0-0-6} times *(see Zeros, page 124)*, every 6th row 0{8-12-8} times, then every 8th row 9{3-0-0} times — 63{67-73-77} sts.

Work even until Sleeve measures 17¹/₂" (44.5 cm), end with a WS row.

Cap Shaping: Bind off 4{4-5-5} sts at the beginning of the next 2 rows — 55{59-63-67} sts.

Next (decrease) Row (RS): SSK *(Figs. 11a-c, page 127)*, work to last 2 sts, K2 tog *(Fig. 8, page 126)*.

Next Row (WS): P1, work in pattern to last st, end P1.

Rep the last 2 rows 15{15-17-18} more times.

Bind off 2 sts at the beginning of the next 2{4-4-2} rows, then 3 sts at beginning of next 0{0-0-2} rows.

Bind off remaining 19 sts.

FINISHING
Sew Fronts to Back at shoulders.

Neckline ribbing: With smaller needles and A, beginning at right Front neck edge, pick up 94 sts evenly around entire neckline edge *(Figs. 13a & b, page 128)*.

Work in K2, P2 rib for 3 rows, change to B for 4 rows, then change to A and work for 2 rows.

Bind off.

Left Front button band: With RS facing and B, pick up 90{94-94-98} sts evenly along entire Front edge.

Work in K2, P2 Rib for 3 rows, change to A for 2 rows, change to B for 2 rows.

Bind off.

Sew 4 buttons evenly spaced, with the lowest button 1¹/₂" (4 cm) from lower edge.

Right Front band: Work as for Left Front band, working 3-st buttonholes opposite buttons on left side (by binding off 3 sts and casting on 3 sts on next row).

Sew Sleeve caps into armholes, easing in any fullness.

Weave Sleeve and side seams *(Fig. 14, page 128)*.

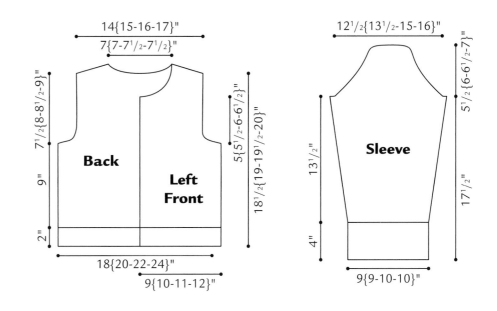

general
INSTRUCTIONS

ABBREVIATIONS

approx.	approximately	FCP	Front Cross Purl	Rnd(s)	Round(s)
BC8	Back Cross 8	FKC	Front Knit Cross	RS	right side
BC	Back Cross	FPC	Front Purl Cross	SSK	slip, slip, knit
BCP	Back Cross Purl	K	knit	St st	Stockinette Stitch
BKC	Back Knit Cross	LH	left hand	st(s)	stitch(es)
BPC	Back Purl Cross	M1	make one	T3B	Twist 3 Back
CC	Contrasting Color	M1-p	make one purlwise	T3F	Twist 3 Front
C5B	Cross 5 Back	MC	Main Color	T4B	Twist 4 Back
C5F	Cross 5 Front	mm	millimeters	T4F	Twist 4 Front
C7B	Cable 7 Back	P	purl	T6B	Twist 6 Back
C7F	Cable 7 Front	PM	place marker	T6F	Twist 6 Front
cm	centimeters	PSSO	pass slipped stitch over	tbl	through back loop
cn	cable needle	rep	repeat	tog	together
dpn(s)	double pointed needle(s)	Rev St st	Reverse Stockinette Stitch	wyib	with yarn in back
				WS	wrong side
FC8	Front Cross 8	RH	right hand	yb	yarn back
FC	Front Cross	RT	Right Twist	yf	yarn forward
				YO	yarn over

* — work instructions following * as many **more** times as indicated in addition to the first time.

( ) or [ ] — work enclosed instructions **as many** times as specified by the number immediately following **or** work all enclosed instructions in the stitch or space indicated **or** contains explanatory remarks.

long dash — the number(s) given after a long dash (—) at the end of a row or round denote(s) the number of stitches you should have on that row or round.

work even — work without increasing or decreasing in the established pattern.

GAUGE

Exact gauge is **essential** for proper fit. Before beginning your project, make a sample swatch in the yarn and needle specified. After completing the swatch, measure it, counting your stitches and rows carefully. If your swatch is larger or smaller than specified, **make another, changing needle size to get the correct gauge**. Keep trying until you find the size needles that will give you the specified gauge. Once proper gauge is obtained, measure width of garment approximately every 3" (7.5 cm) to be sure gauge remains consistent.

HINTS

As in all garments, good finishing techniques make a big difference in the quality of the piece. Do not tie knots. Always start a new ball at the beginning of a row, leaving ends long enough to weave in later. With **wrong** side facing, weave the needle through several stitches, then reverse the direction and weave it back through several stitches. When the ends are secure, clip them off close to the work.

KNITTING NEEDLES		
UNITED STATES	ENGLISH U.K.	METRIC (mm)
0	13	2
1	12	2.25
2	11	2.75
3	10	3.25
4	9	3.5
5	8	3.75
6	7	4
7	6	4.5
8	5	5
9	4	5.5
10	3	6
10½	2	6.5
11	1	8
13	00	9
15	000	10
17	---	12.75

KNIT TERMINOLOGY	
UNITED STATES	INTERNATIONAL
gauge =	tension
bind off =	cast off
yarn over (YO) =	yarn forward (yfwd) **or** yarn around needle (yrn)

Yarn Weight Symbol & Names	LACE 0	SUPER FINE 1	FINE 2	LIGHT 3	MEDIUM 4	BULKY 5	SUPER BULKY 6
Type of Yarns in Category	Fingering, size 10 crochet thread	Sock, Fingering, Baby	Sport, Baby	DK, Light Worsted	Worsted, Afghan, Aran	Chunky, Craft, Rug	Bulky, Roving
Knit Gauge Range* in Stockinette St to 4" (10 cm)	33-40** sts	27-32 sts	23-26 sts	21-24 sts	16-20 sts	12-15 sts	6-11 sts
Advised Needle Size Range	000-1	1 to 3	3 to 5	5 to 7	7 to 9	9 to 11	11 and larger

*GUIDELINES ONLY: The chart above reflects the most commonly used gauges and needle sizes for specific yarn categories.

** Lace weight yarns are usually knitted on larger needles to create lacy openwork patterns. Accordingly, a gauge range is difficult to determine. Always follow the gauge stated in your pattern.

◖☐☐☐ BEGINNER	Projects for first-time knitters using basic knit and purl stitches. Minimal shaping.
◖◖☐☐ EASY	Projects using basic stitches, repetitive stitch patterns, simple color changes, and simple shaping and finishing.
◖◖◖☐ INTERMEDIATE	Projects with a variety of stitches, such as basic cables and lace, simple intarsia, double-pointed needles and knitting in the round needle techniques, mid-level shaping and finishing.
◖◖◖◖ EXPERIENCED	Projects using advanced techniques and stitches, such as short rows, fair isle, more intricate intarsia, cables, lace patterns, and numerous color changes.

ZEROS

To consolidate the length of an involved pattern, Zeros are sometimes used so that all sizes can be combined. For example, knit 0{1-2} sts means the first size would do nothing, the second size would K1, and the largest size would K2.

MARKERS

As a convenience to you, we have used markers to help distinguish the beginning of a pattern or round or to mark placement of decreases or increases. Place markers as instructed. You may use purchased markers or tie a length of contrasting color yarn around the needle. When you reach a marker on each row or round, slip it from the left needle to the right needle; remove it when no longer needed.

FAIR ISLE KNITTING

Fair Isle Knitting is a Stockinette Stitch technique that uses two colors across a row.

CHANGING COLORS

Drop the color you are using, lay the other color to your left on top of it, pick up the color you were using and continue working. The unused color is attached to the fabric *(Fig. 1a)*.

Fig. 1a

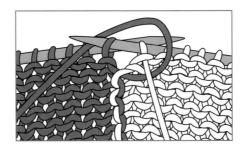

STRANDING

Stranding is the method in which the color not in use is carried across the **wrong** side of the fabric *(Fig. 1b)*. It gives a nice appearance on the right side and also provides added warmth.

Fig. 1b

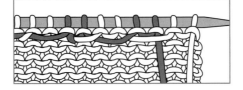

If the strands are carried more than an inch, it can be difficult to keep tension. The strands can be easily snagged when putting the garment on or pulling it off. To avoid carrying the yarn across 5 stitches, twist the carried color at its midpoint with the yarn in use. Make sure the carried yarn doesn't show on the right side or tighten the tension.

FOLLOWING A CHART

Designs for Fair Isle knitting are worked from a chart. It is easier to follow a chart than written instructions and you can also see what the pattern looks like. The chart shows each stitch as a square indicating what color each stitch should be. Visualize the chart as your fabric, beginning at the bottom edge. Work as follows: on **right** side rows, follow the chart from **right** to **left**; on **wrong** side rows, follow the chart from **left** to **right**.

For ease in following the chart, place a ruler on the chart over the row being worked to help keep your place.

USING DOUBLE POINTED NEEDLES

When working too few stitches to use a circular needle, double pointed needles are required. Divide the stitches into fourths and slip one-fourth of the stitches onto each of 4 double pointed needles *(Fig. 2)*, forming a square. With the fifth needle, knit across the stitches on the first needle. You will now have an empty needle with which to knit the stitches from the next needle. Work the first stitch of each needle firmly to prevent gaps.

Fig. 2

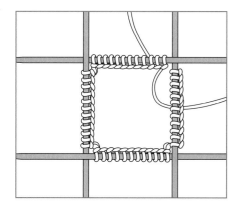

YARN OVER
(abbreviated YO)

Bring the yarn forward **between** the needles, then back **over** the top of the right hand needle, so that it is now in position to knit the next stitch *(Fig. 3)*.

Fig. 3

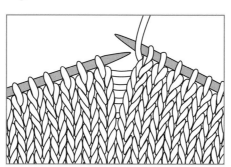

KNIT THROUGH THE BACK LOOP
(abbreviated tbl)

Insert the right needle into the **back** of next stitch from **front** to **back** *(Fig. 4)*, then **knit** the stitch.

Fig. 4

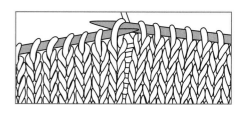

INCREASES

The type of increase used depends on the stitch needed to maintain the pattern.

BAR INCREASE

The bar increase uses one stitch to make two stitches. You will have two stitches on the right needle for the one stitch worked off the left needle.

Knit the next stitch but do **not** slip the old stitch off the left needle **(Fig. 5a)**. Insert the right needle into the **back** loop of the **same** stitch and knit it **(Fig. 5b)**, then slip the old stitch off the left needle.

Fig. 5a

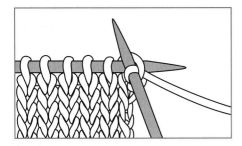

Fig. 5b

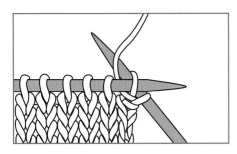

MAKE 1 *(abbreviated M1)*

Insert the **left** needle under the horizontal strand between the stitches from the **front (Fig. 6a)**. Then knit into the **back** of the strand *(Fig. 6b)*.

Fig. 6a

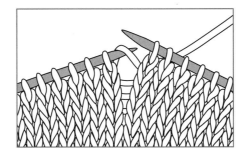

Fig. 6b

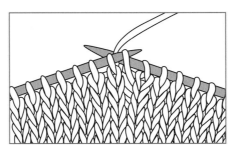

MAKE 1 PURLWISE
(abbreviated M1-p)

Insert the **left** needle under the horizontal strand between the stitches from the **front** *(Fig. 7)*. Then purl into the **back** of the strand.

Fig. 7

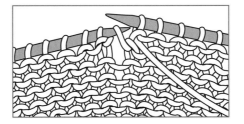

INCREASING OR DECREASING EVENLY ACROSS A ROW

Add one to the number of increases/decreases required and divide that number into the number of stitches on the needle. Subtract one from the result and the new number is the approximate number of stitches to be worked between each increase/decrease. Adjust the number as needed.

DECREASES
KNIT 2 TOGETHER
(abbreviated K2 tog)

Insert the right needle into the **front** of the first two stitches on the left needle as if to **knit** *(Fig. 8)*, then **knit** them together as if they were one stitch.

Fig. 8

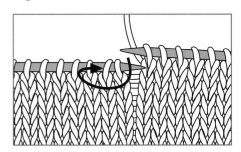

PURL 2 TOGETHER
(abbreviated P2 tog)
Insert the right needle into the **front** of the first two stitches on the left needle as if to **purl** *(Fig. 9)*, then **purl** them together as if they were one stitch.

Fig. 9

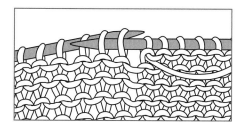

PURL 2 TOGETHER THROUGH THE BACK LOOP *(abbreviated P2 tog tbl)*
Insert the right needle into the **back** of both stitches from **back** to **front** *(Fig. 10)*, then **purl** them together.

Fig. 10

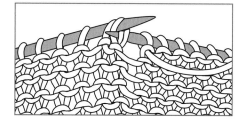

SLIP, SLIP, KNIT
(abbreviated SSK)
Separately slip two stitches as if to **knit** *(Fig. 11a)*. Insert the **left** needle into the **front** of both slipped stitches *(Fig. 11b)* and then **knit** them together as if they were one stitch *(Fig. 11c)*.

Fig. 11a

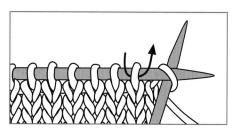

Fig. 11b

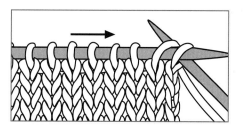

Fig. 11c

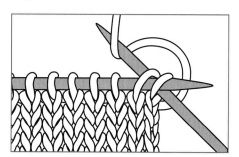

SLIP 1, KNIT 2 TOGETHER, PASS SLIPPED STITCH OVER
(abbreviated slip 1, K2 tog, PSSO)
Slip one stitch as if to **knit** *(Fig. 12a)*, then knit the next two stitches together *(Fig. 8, page 126)*. With the left needle, bring the slipped stitch over the stitch just made *(Fig. 12b)* and off the needle.

Fig. 12a

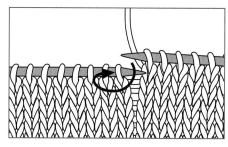

Fig. 12b

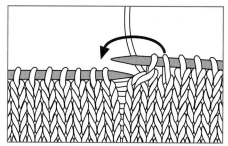

PICKING UP STITCHES

When instructed to pick up stitches, insert the needle from the **front** to the **back** under two strands at the edge of the worked piece *(Figs. 13a & b)*. Put the yarn around the needle as if to **knit**, then bring the needle with the yarn back through the stitch to the right side, resulting in a stitch on the needle.

Repeat this along the edge, picking up the required number of stitches.

A crochet hook may be helpful to pull yarn through.

Fig. 13a

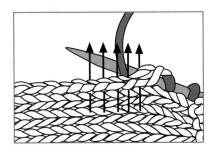

Fig. 13b

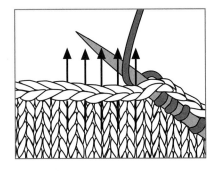

WEAVING SEAMS

With the **right** side of both pieces facing you and edges even, sew through both sides once to secure the seam. Insert the needle under the bar **between** the first and second stitches on the row and pull the yarn through *(Fig. 14)*. Insert the needle under the next bar on the second side. Repeat from side to side, being careful to match rows. If the edges are different lengths, it may be necessary to insert the needle under two bars at one edge.

Fig. 14